academic

financial

personal

geographic

THE
HONEYCOMB
APPROACH

6 Factors to Find Your College Fit

emotional

social

Also by Joann Korte Elliott:

When to Do What:
A Step-by-Step Guide to the College Process

THE HONEYCOMB APPROACH

6 Factors to Find Your College Fit

CCT

College Counseling Tutoring, LLC
"It's all about FIT"

Joann Korte Elliott

LCCN: 2019915630
ISBN-13: 978-0-9991065-1-8

Dedication

This book is dedicated to the memory of my parents. I still miss you every day. I hope you are proud of who I've become.

Contents

Foreword

You may hope this book you hold in your hands is about *how* to get into college. If so, you will be disappointed. **This book is about finding your *why*.** It's about figuring out what you want. This book is about a holistic and healthy approach to college. There is no Utopia University. There is no slam dunk. There is no 1-800-GET-ME-IN number you can dial. Finding a college that is right for you is a unique process different from everyone else's. After 25-plus years working in the college counseling field, no one student or family I have worked with has ever had a seamless, perfect college search experience without a hurdle, obstacle, setback, or disappointment at some point in their journey. The key to finding a great college for YOU is considering all sides of this process—not just academic and financial—to find a school that will help you grow into who you are meant to be.

Students and parents are getting the wrong message about college. From the pressure under which students operate, the competitive nature from which they find their motivation, to their sense of entitlement that comes from having 'arrived' upon being admitted to a top-notch school, we are sending a message that college is a finish line—an end. In fact, it is just one brief stop on the journey that is your life. It can be a pivotal and influential stop, but not a definitive end. It is not the cherry on top of the sundae. So why are we so caught up in where everyone is admitted to college? Perhaps, it is the parents' benchmark by which they gauge their success. If their child has good grades, checked the boxes, and goes to School "X", they as parents have raised a wonderful child. Maybe it's a fear that if their child doesn't go to a top-notch school that the chance for future success is greatly diminished. Or, maybe it is the student's attempt at being worthy enough of love and acceptance as a result of their accomplishments instead of their mere existence. In any case, these are not healthy approaches to the college search process. I've learned that during the college search process people often bypass their intuition and common sense all for the sake of worrying 'what will people think?' Chances are, people are so wrapped up in their own drama they don't even care about yours. Or, if they do gossip about you it's probably to make themselves feel better. Which, in the end, is way more about *them* than *you*. I think it's time to focus on what's right for YOUR situation rather than caring what others think. Stop following the crowd. Don't give others the power to decide what success looks like for YOU. We are so much more than where we go to college. We are the sum of our parts and college is only one part of who we are.

It seems from my vantage point we are putting our emphasis for success on the wrong things. Our society focuses on college as a status symbol, but the truth is we have a massive mental health crisis on our hands. We are broken. Flawed. Anxious. We need to consider this reality when choosing a college. **A school whose name correlates with 'a good education' doesn't necessarily serve you in other ways—personally, socially, emotionally, or financially, for example.** And, if we are the sum of our parts, why are we only considering a portion of who we are when selecting a college that will be our home for the next four years? **I think it's time we have a book about how to choose a college that supports you on various levels—including emotionally and socially—and less about how to get into a certain school.**

We must look past the obvious surface considerations when choosing a college. Aspects like the financial and academic pieces are key components of this decision-making process. But they aren't the only two sides to consider. Perhaps if we took a collective look at all the sides that matter in the college search process, we might see a deeper success with our students entering (and finishing) college. It's a well-documented statistic that a significant number of students who start college will never finish. If you want to lessen the chance that you will be a college dropout, do the hard work now to know yourself, how you operate, and what scenarios will help you succeed. **It requires a great deal of maturity to be able to distinguish between what you *want* and what you *need*.** If you are that student who seeks a well-rounded, challenging, fulfilling college experience then I encourage you to read this book along with your parents and find your *why* in each category—there are six—and **find your fit** that will move you forward towards the next best step in your future.

I hope that reading this book will prompt conversation within families that moves everyone toward a well-defined and thought-out college decision they can make *together*. College is so much more than just name-brand schools, grades, status, and test scores. It is personal, unique, and an adventure waiting to unfold if you're willing to do the hard work to know yourself and be honest about what is best for you at this point in your life.

I also hope this book can accomplish two things. First, I hope it encourages readers to listen to their gut and to be proud of their decisions. Well-informed decisions made by looking at all sides and considering all angles are usually good ones. But even then, there is no guarantee. There is no one right or guaranteed path to success—college included. Life is a process. It is steps and missteps, decisions and mistakes. **Learn to embrace those mistakes. They are great teachers for future success.** Missteps and mistakes make us stronger if we learn the lesson they present. Sometimes we all make mistakes or wish we'd chosen another path. But learning to listen to our intuition and trusting our gut can go a long way in helping us make better decisions. Many strategies and approaches outlined in this book can be used for any decision in life—not just for choosing a college.

Second, this book is designed to be thought-provoking. It is designed to prompt thought and reflection and to consider if there's a better way to arrive at the decision before you. You will find a few questions at the end of each chapter that will encourage you to stop and consider all the angles and 'what if's' as you ponder what might be your next best step. Use them as a journal entry to write about or just roll some new ideas around in your head for a while. Either works as it will provide you with insight into your decision-making process and help you decide what you want and what fits YOU best.

Whatever decision you are about to make regarding college, make it with your own best interest for the long haul, front and center. Many of us feel pressure to name drop or, even worse, apologize for our educational background. There seems to be a mindset over the last 20 years or so that where you go to college is somehow a guarantee of who you will become in your life or that you are a good person and it's simply not true. I hate to break it to you, but the only way to become a great person is to be a great person. No school can make you that. Only you can do that. The same is true for success as well. We control our successes through our work ethic and not by where we went to college! That fact, though, should be empowering! **As you read this book, I encourage you to become empowered by asking yourself not "where will I go to college?" but, rather, "who will I become?".**

Changing Perspective

D o you remember the picture of the dress that stormed the internet a few years back? The one where no one could agree on whether the dress was gold and white or blue and black? It sparked quite a debate online. In the end, it came down to perception. Things like lighting and neuroscience were credited with creating the perception of the color variances. Just like that dress, our perception of college is seen differently. Today, our perception of college is that applying and being admitted is more stressful than years past. But why? This perception can be attributed to a wide variety of factors including technological advances. These advances may have made the process of applying easier but has also provided students with an endless array of college options that can overwhelm the senses. In students' quest to find the 'perfect' college, there has also been a shift to focus on college as a status symbol. We no longer focus on why a certain college is a good fit for us but, rather, consume ourselves with how attending a certain college makes us look to the rest of the world. We focus on *where* to go to college and *how* to get there and have forgotten to ask ourselves *why* we're making the choices we are. These shifts in perception are creating a lot of pressure for students and their families. Just like a turn of a kaleidoscope can shift perception, so can a turn in our world. In our world, the perception of college and what it means to be successful has turned and not necessarily for the better.

When I began working in the college counseling profession, things were more black-and-white. Things that mattered were largely pragmatic and what I like to call the 3 P's: price, program, and proximity. People were concerned with the cost of the institution (usually looking for the best deal), making sure the college had the program the student wanted to study and was in reasonable proximity to home. The students and families I worked with were concerned about the basics. They looked at a handful of schools and made a rather decisive choice in a relatively short amount of time. This was nearly 30 years ago. Those were simpler times. And while there were always those students (even 30 years ago) for whom the college process was riddled with pressure from parents to achieve success and status, many students took a more deliberate approach. The college admission process was not especially stressful. Besides deciding on a major, what probably provided the most stress for students was the paperwork it took to get it all finished. All applications were hard copies, completed by hand in blue or black ink. The application with all its supplemental materials (essay, activity list, check for the application fee, etc.) was given to the college counselor at the high school who added to the packet letters of recommendation and a high school transcript and off it went to the post office. I remember carrying armfuls of envelopes to the school's main office and standing for inordinate amounts of time in front of the postage meter weighing and stamping packets that would eventually determine everyone's futures.

This was a far cry from today's world. Because we live in these times, we forget the frenzied pace at which our world has accelerated in the past 20 years. Technological developments such as the internet, email, scanning, YouTube, online applications, Skype, iPhones, and texting are just a few things that have drastically changed the scope and speed by which one chooses a college. When you consider technological changes such as these it may appear the college admission process is easier now than ever.

Gone are the days of putting papers into envelopes and (heaven forbid) snail mailing them to the college. Everything is completed online. Only a handful of schools even offer a paper application anymore and the only reason that exists is to accommodate students whose homes or schools simply do not have internet access. Even the Common Application, an online application system accepted by a few hundred colleges and counting at the time, was also done by paper. You filled out one application and made copies of it to send to the other schools that accepted the Common Application. This is in sharp contrast to today's Common Application accepted by nearly 900 colleges and universities and has approximately one million students using it each year to submit over five million applications! The application, while still requiring you to provide many pieces of information, makes it to your college of choice in record time simply by hitting submit. This alone encourages students to apply to more schools by the simplistic nature of clicking, copying and pasting, entering a credit card number, and hitting submit. No paper necessary. Add to this the ease at which test scores and transcripts are submitted electronically and it all seems a breeze. With all the speed and convenience of technology, who needs patience? We have the internet.

Want to visit a college, but don't have the time? The internet can take care of that. YouTube videos, interactive college tour programs, and college websites can all make you feel you are there experiencing the real thing even if you are having only a virtual experience. You can save yourself hours of time driving or flying to an unfamiliar destination by just a few searches online. You can read hours of reviews by students and families about their experiences and shared judgments of a variety of institutions. And, you can do this all from the comfort of your own home!

And, finally, there's no need to worry about missing anyone away at college. Technological advances including email, social media, texting, cell phones, and Skype all make it so convenient and instantaneous for us to stay in constant contact with our loved ones. There is no need to worry about someone being halfway across the country. Gone are the days of dropping a student off at college never to be seen or heard from again until the semester's end. Instead, parents and students are often in daily conversation from across the country or even across the world.

You would think with all these technological advances we would be set. College choice and the work to apply should be seamless, easy, convenient. If so, then why are we so stressed about this process? We have, thanks to technology, widened our perspective of what is available to us with college choice. And while there are aspects of this that are, undoubtedly, good, the fact is that technology has overwhelmed our senses. Maybe we have too many options. With so many more available options from which to choose simply by sheer exposure and knowledge of their existence, students feel more pressure than ever to get it right. That pressure is felt in many ways from searching coast to coast for the perfect school, buying into the idea of there being one 'right' school, and applying to a multitude of colleges 'just in case.' That last idea consists largely of throwing everything at the wall and seeing what sticks.

We are bombarded by messages that colleges are more difficult to get into than ever. Some of that message is true. With the ease of applying to numerous schools with just a little more effort than it is to apply to just a handful, students will often apply everywhere just to avoid the overwhelming decision of choosing a handful that will be a good fit. In doing so, the number of applications at each institution goes up and they, in turn, appear to have a lower acceptance rate because the number of applications is exceedingly higher than the number of spots they have available. This creates a dilemma for the admissions staff too as they try to sift through all the applications trying to find the best candidates who want to be at their school and separate those applications from those who applied everywhere just to see what stuck. At this point, it becomes stressful for everyone whether you're a student, parent, counselor, or admission rep. Our ease of technology is sometimes making this process more stressful and more overwhelming.

Technology has also created a 'kid in a candy store' experience as well. Inundated with the endless option of colleges from which to choose, students and their families often grasp for everything within reach (or not in reach) when searching for a college. This creates a 'more is more' mindset and, for some, a 'keeping up with the Joneses' mentality creating financial stress as well. Our society has instilled in us a FOMO attitude (Fear of Missing Out, for those of you acronymically challenged). This has been influenced by social media and everyone's seemingly picture-perfect posts and tweets. In the end, some people find themselves lost, unsettled, and unfocused on what they truly want. In all our abundance, we have come up poor. We are overwhelmed, exasperated, and exhausted.

As the world of college admissions expanded because of technology, parents and students sought more information about the college process to get a 'leg up' as they pursued a wider range of schools. There was an increase in demand for information about the college admission process—the *how* if you will. How do I apply? How do I find the best college for biology majors? How do I get in? High school counseling centers answered that request for information with college nights, college fairs, summer camps to complete college applications, college bus tours, financial aid nights... anything that would educate families on *how* to get into college. It was a never-ending demand and unquenchable thirst for information. Understanding that process is important, yes. It is crucial to understand timelines, deadlines, and the process overall. Failure to do so can cause missed opportunities, but how to get into college is only part of the process. **Over time, students and families became obsessed with the *where* and the *how* in the college process. But what we forgot about was the *why*.** Understanding the *how* may get students into college, but it's understanding the *why* that keeps them there.

It's not enough to be consumed by understanding the *how* of the college process, we must also know our reasons for seeking college in the first place. **We need to shift our perception from only sharing the factual aspects of the college process *(how)* to focusing on the needs of the student *(why)*.** Most people are unaware that less than 40 percent of students who start college will finish in 4 years. By the time 6 years have passed, only 60 percent of students finished a 4-year degree. That means 40 percent of students who start college will never finish with 75 percent of those dropping out by the end of freshmen year. That we are seeing so many students not thrive even in their first year at college begs us to ask the question why? Why, if students are accepted into a university, are they not staying? What factors are contributing to them returning home? Why are they not thriving? What support systems are not in place for them to come full circle to complete their post-secondary education or training? These are good questions that demand answers.

The perception is that getting into college is stressful, but what people are not grasping is that the stress associated with the college admission process is just the tip of the iceberg. The stress that comes from getting into college is often elongated and permeates the entire educational experience from the moment they enter high school (sometimes earlier) until they graduate college or drop out. Whether self-imposed or under the watchful eye of well-meaning parents, the stress is real.

It seems the college admission process has become so hyped up with a mindset that students must hit certain benchmarks, volunteer incessantly, or have test scores that rival Einstein's as a prerequisite to gain admission to college. Our focus has become one-sided. We only consider the academic piece of the admission puzzle when preparing students for college. But, if we are the sum of our parts, we need to consider who we are, not only academically, but psychologically as well. An experience I had when preparing for a presentation recently caused a major paradigm shift for me on why we must take a more holistic approach to the college process rather than just an academic focus. We need to shift our perception of what 'college' and 'success' look like.

A few years back, I was asked to address a regional parent group about the stress kids were under while applying to college. In preparing my talk, I reached out to several of my colleagues still working as high school counselors. I asked them to share with their student bodies a short survey I had designed and asked them to complete it. The goal was to get 'from the horse's mouth' what their feelings were on the topic. Students were told clearly at the beginning of the survey that if they felt excessively stressed or overwhelmed or especially if they had thoughts of suicide to contact the prevention hotline using the phone number provided at the top of the survey. This may seem extreme, but as a therapist, I knew it was important for people to have somewhere to turn if they found themselves in a dangerous low spot. Because the surveys were anonymous and I would have no way to access the student or the ability to get them the help if they needed it, I needed to provide outside assistance should they need support. I thought my attention to detail might be too extreme, but as I read the results of the surveys, I found myself in shock over what I had stumbled upon. While no one had expressed thoughts of ending their life or a sense of hopelessness in their survey responses, I was taken back by the sad messages they left.

About 100 students completed the survey. This was far less than the total number who were asked to participate. I probably got back about 10 percent of the student population chosen. But that 10 percent had a lot to say. In survey after survey, I read messages from frustrated and, quite honestly, sad students getting strong messages about their performance in high school and the connection to their future and their sense of worth as a son or daughter in the eyes of their parent(s) based on the outcome of those efforts. The questions asked weren't just about the college process itself. Students were also asked about their toughest adjustment to high school socially and academically and how parents increased or decreased that stress.

Their responses were honest, funny, heartbreaking, and transparent. I was not prepared for the responses I got. They were very forthcoming and revealing. What I was impressed with was how well these students had their finger on the pulse of their feelings. They knew what the issues were. Heck, some even knew they were the issue! I applauded their vulnerability and honesty. As part of the survey, I also had asked them if they could say anything to a roomful of parents about stress in high school, what would they tell them? I got an earful. But I kept good on my promise I made to them at the beginning of the survey: that I was speaking to a roomful of parents from all over the city and I was their messenger so tell me what you need them to know. So I did. And some parents were caught off-guard as I read the comments.

I could tell some were taken aback by the messages the kids were hearing and the audacity of what things parents said to their kids. I could hear an almost imperceptible slinking down in the seats as some heard their own words repeated back to them. I could see by the surprised looks that people had no idea their kid (or anyone else's kid) felt this bad about high school in general—be it academically or socially—let alone the college process. I had certainly gotten their attention. And those students had gotten mine.

My presentation went on and we talked about other aspects of this topic as well as ways to maybe right the ship or re-word conversations. I left them with one piece of homework of their own to do that night. I told them to go home, find their kid, get them to look up from their screen, and tell them that they loved them. That no matter the past or the future, that they unconditionally loved them for who they are. Right here. Right now. They were loved by Mom and/or Dad. Warts and all.

I have no idea how the homework went. It wasn't graded by me. There was no reporting back. I guess the true grade came from the outcome. If it inspired a breakthrough conversation or a truce, I suppose they'd get an A. If it didn't work wonders, but they were still all trying then they probably deserved an A+. Because trying is sometimes more important than anything. There's nothing harder than getting knocked down and getting back up and trying again. Teens won't be teens forever. Memories about GPAs and test scores fade, but everyone remembers conversations that sting. They will outgrow this 'phase' they're in. It's part of human development. But a parent losing a kid's trust, love, or admiration because they harp on things that rarely matter isn't worth it. Students remember those conversations long after the biology grade was forgotten. The bottom line in all of this is that our perception of college has changed. It has moved from being viewed as an opportunity for a better future to an overwhelming, pressure-filled obligation for everyone who contemplates 'success'. What we have forgotten, though, is that the path to success is as varied as the individuals who strive for it.

Everyone starts from a different place in life. Some of us are more financially privileged than others. Others of us are more intellectually privileged. Some of us have problems at home or emotional issues to consider. Everyone has a different starting block. And there is a different path for everyone. Even within the same family, it is not uncommon for siblings to choose very different paths. We need to take a holistic look at the college process and decide based on our unique situations (with no apologies) and make the best decision for ourselves rather than what we think we *should* do, or what others think we should do. **The Honeycomb Approach encourages everyone to do that— take a hexagonal approach to the college process and consider <u>six</u> individual perspectives we need to examine to make a smart decision for life after high school.** I believe we inherently have a hunch, an intuition about what we should be doing with our lives. It just takes courage to listen to it. Considering all six sides of the hexagon can be a gut check for every student that they are on the right path and provide you with the courage to step forward to make the best decision possible for your future.

Understanding
the Honeycomb Approach

You might be wondering what the Honeycomb Approach is or what a beehive might have to do with making a good college or life choice. Have you ever educated yourself about bees? Bees are amazing creatures. It's no surprise where the phrase "worker bee" came from. The exquisite work that bees do to produce such a light and yet strong product as the honeycomb is impressive.

One day I was watching a video about organic honey versus manufactured (synthetic) honey. In the video, they said that authentic honey would keep a honeycomb pattern if you put some water in it and spun it around. You could see the honeycomb pattern in the honey itself. The genetic makeup of the honey would reveal a honeycomb pattern reflective of the hive in which it was created. This was opposed to the synthetic honey produced on an assembly line (manmade) that would simply look like a blob of sugar and water when spun together. Authenticity was reflected in the honey created by bees. I was so impressed by the intricate detail of this. So, it got me thinking, what makes a honeycomb so remarkable? Aside from its exquisite and detailed pattern, honeycombs are strong and yet amazingly lightweight. If you've ever picked up a honeycomb created by a bee, it is very air-like and feels fragile, yet is incredibly resilient. How is it that a creature as simple and fragile as a bee can instinctively create such a strong and intricate masterpiece? **The key to a honeycomb's resilient nature is in its simple design—a hexagon. That simple six-sided figure that, when placed one next to the other, creates a STRONG and RESILIENT pattern that, when placed one upon the other creates a dynamic and sturdy force.** Hexagons, like the honeycombs created by bees, are the strongest way to create a structure by creating the most efficient use of space all while using the least amount of materials. These bees are working SMART. Hexagons are evident in many aspects of nature from honeycombs to snowflakes and even organic compounds.

The brilliant design of a honeycomb has been replicated by man in many other designs including shipping boxes for much of the same reason bees use honeycombs to protect their hives. For bees, their lightweight, but strong design is key to making sure their honey is protected while for humans, a honeycomb-designed shipping box makes sure your Amazon orders arrive protected and intact. **This perfect creation got me to thinking: what if I took the concept of a honeycomb—that brilliantly designed six-sided figure—and applied the concept to something intangible like the college search?** It may seem farfetched but bear with me.

When we consider how we make choices regarding colleges, we often look at only one or maybe two factors for consideration. We might look at the cost (financial) to attend the college or the rigor and notoriety of the institution (academic), but we are neglecting so many other facets that must go into this decision to make it work.

By taking a multi-disciplined approach to college, it goes a long way to ensure that students' needs, abilities, and circumstances are all considered in a holistic effort when choosing a college.

It's important when we look at colleges that we ask ourselves *why* we want certain attributes as it relates to the honeycomb approach. *Why* do we want a certain geographic location? *Why* do we want certain academic programs? *Why* is this school a good social or emotional fit for me? *Why* will this college be a good fit financially in my ability to pay off debt or have a higher quality of life after graduation? *Why* am I drawn personally to consider this school?

In my graduate school counseling program, they taught us not to ask 'why' of a client. We were taught it implied justification by the client to explain themselves often putting people on the defensive. In the college admission process, though, it is important to ask people what their *why* is. We must challenge people to think through their decision-making process, consider all the angles, and make certain their reasons are strong. Trust me, you can look at this decision from all the angles and still not get it right, but your chances of success go up the more effort you put into looking at all sides that factor into the decision BEFORE you make it.

Many students today are bouncing back from college no degree in hand. They are not finishing college for a variety of reasons. Some of it is due to financial constraints while other reasons include rigor or even mental health issues. Because we look at the college process as so one-dimensional, other factors that can cause a student not to succeed are overlooked and yet can derail even the smartest, most capable student from achieving a college degree. Until we look at the college process and what truly FITS a student as a multi-faceted or hexagonal approach and consider all sides, all factors in this choice, problems regarding student satisfaction and success will continue.

The college experience is not a 'one size fits all' experience.

In using the honeycomb approach, we consider six major factors when helping teens decide their next logical step in pursuing their post-secondary education. These six factors work together to form a holistic approach to finding a great-fitting college for the student. When we look at the process from a more holistic standpoint, there are six sides to the college hexagon.

These are:

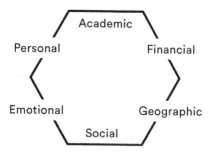

Using the analogy of the honeycomb, utilizing all six factors listed above allows our intangible hexagon to provide a strong foundation on which to build each student's future. Throughout the rest of this book, we will delve into each side of the hexagon and seek to understand why each component should factor into the college decision-making process. Creating strong students can only happen when we consider all sides. Considering only one (or a few) of the components will make the honeycomb incomplete, weak, lopsided, and prone to collapse. Have you ever seen a bee construct a triangle or square-shaped hive? No. Because bees instinctively do what works. Hexagon upon hexagon produces a strong and vibrant result. When students jet off to college following the crowd, ignoring financial factors or emotional needs, they often boomerang home. They end up right where they started. This is often because some important aspect of who they are or what needs they have has been neglected. At this point, their world crumbles. They are unprepared for college on some level in the environment they chose. These 'boomerang' students often turn up in my office feeling bad about themselves and wanting a do-over. Little by little, we unpack what went wrong and re-direct. Using the honeycomb approach ensures a firm foundation on which to build a future whether for a soon-to-be college student or a young adult wanting a second chance at their education.

Imagine, now, if the hexagon represents one child and all the many parts listed above make up each side of their honeycomb. **Considering all six areas will produce strong, resilient, and competent people capable of being problem-solving, thriving, and successful individuals.** Now, take it one step further. Imagine each hexagon representing each child stacked one next to and upon another. Imagine what a fortress of strength, fortitude, and resources we could produce if we only looked at the college process as holistic and not just "where did you go to college"? **Perhaps the more important question is not "where did you go?", but rather, "who did you become?"** Imagine a society where every child, by whatever means and resources fit them, could make for themselves a better life. From a societal standpoint, this means a better life for all of us. To take a holistic approach involves depth, self-analysis, honesty, and vulnerability. It's not the easy way out. It's finding what fits THE STUDENT and having the courage to walk that path that leads to the future that will make them the very best version of themselves.

Full Disclosure

Before I dig into the various sides of the hexagon in more detail, I think it's only fair I divulge my educational path. Full disclosure: my educational path after high school was uncertain, messy, and some might even say undesirable. I prefer to call it a hot mess. It sounds better. But I put it before you so you can see I don't have all the answers. There was not (and still isn't) this crystal clear, smooth path that is 'right.' Like I said before, life is a series of missteps and mistakes. I was no exception to that in my personal journey. However, I think we can agree that knowledge is power. The more we look at all the sides of the decision-making process, the more likely we are to make a smart, informed decision that serves us well as individuals without considering (or caring) what anyone else thinks. Looking back, I can see I cared way too much about what other people thought. Not so much at the time of making my educational choices, but after the fact. I was the one who found myself ashamed of my less-than-impressive path and failure to enroll at a name-brand institution that would impress at the networking happy hour. In the end, though, my journey was mine and I needed to own it. It was through an experience after college that reminded me I needed to own my story and not apologize for it. **When we know better, we do better.**

● ○ ● ○ ●

The best part of my job is watching my students from wherever in life they come to begin planning for the next step. Whether they come from money or not, have book smarts or not, overcome adversity or not—it doesn't matter. I am equally enthusiastic for the kid who 'has it all' as the one who barely passed math. It's a tremendous feeling and one of the greatest sources of joy in my career. I don't judge their starting block—financially, academically, emotionally. It doesn't matter where they come from. The important part is that they are moving forward. **It is in our moving forward we create upward mobility.** But none of us like to be judged by whatever starting block we come from, myself included. For me, however, I found myself on the receiving end of judgment sitting in my own office long after my formal education had commenced.

One morning, two parents of a bright, ambitious junior sat in my office with their daughter in tow. As we settled in for the next hour to discuss college plans and so I could help answer questions they had, I was prepared as I had met with hundreds of families before. But I was not as prepared for the conversation as I thought. Shortly after the conversation began, the mom asked me where I went to college. It's not the first time anyone's asked me that. It is natural curiosity given the topic at hand. I never mind the question and I usually perceive their question as complimentary as they take an interest in this stranger that sits before them. (I recognize that's naïve and they may instead be assessing my credentials.)

My response to her was that I went two years to the community college and transferred my associate degree to a four-year private college in town. I'd majored in Business Administration. I followed up with where I'd gotten my master's in education (counseling) which was a local, in-town public university. My answer was straightforward. No explanation. No shame. Just facts. Her response floored and humiliated me. She cocked her head to the right, made a little face, and gave a pitiful, sympathy-dripping response of "Oh, that's okay." She was trying to console me! Her verbal response, along with the tone of her voice and the non-verbal cues she elicited, was like nails on a chalkboard. It oozed with insincerity and pity. It was condescending. I could feel the blood rush to my neck and head. I was so angry and felt so diminished by her. And, to have her child witness this put-down of me was undermining. My mind was racing.

To right the ship and not let her see she had upset me, I took a deep breath and calmly responded, "I know." I left it at that. I didn't owe this woman an explanation for anything. Her patronizing comment was not worthy of a response. She didn't know my starting block. She had no idea what circumstances in life I had come from or what strides I had made. How dare she! But then I thought better of my anger. Her ignorance was not my problem. I was proud of the hard work I had done and where I'd gotten in life. It didn't matter what she thought about how I made my decisions along the way. While I quickly wrapped my brain around my position on this in a matter of seconds as a not-so-wet-behind-the-ears thirty-some-thing, I can't imagine what damage is done when these things are said to teens. From putting down test scores: "You'll do better next time" or "Why can't you be more like your brother?" or "If you don't get an A in this class, you can kiss college goodbye", I have to wonder what damage we are doing to students mentally. The truth is there is more than one way to get to the airport. Why can't there be more than one way to get to college? It's all dependent on your perspective. **You wouldn't take the same route to the airport as someone who lived at the opposite end of the city. Why would you ever take someone else's perspective when finding the right path for your college education?**

As for me, had that mother had a little perspective and background on my personal life perhaps she would've been less judgmental and patronizing. My own college experience is so bizarrely disorganized it seems ironic, even to me, that I do what I do for a living. But like us all, I am a survivor and I got here. It's not who crosses the finish line first or wears the best running shoes. It is the mere fact that we stay the course and run our own race that counts. And I did.

I was always a good student. I got good grades and good test scores. I never really struggled. I enjoyed learning and liked being in school. I loved helping others and the camaraderie that school provided. High school, though, had its challenges like it does for most of us. There was probably a little less emphasis on grades and learning and probably a little too much on figuring out who I was and worrying about what my peers thought all while trying to fit in. However, I got through remarkably unscathed and in good standing academically. I was no valedictorian, but my innate ability and work ethic gave me the means to handle a part-time job working 20 hours a week year-round and still pull A's and B's on my report cards.

As my senior year was unfolding, there was plenty of uncertainty about what would come next. Like most students I had ideas of what I might do but, largely, there was no exit plan. I knew I was interested in pursuing college. I wanted to go away—not too far—and I thought I wanted a smaller school. I was interested in education and considered becoming an elementary teacher. Like most students, I was swayed by what everyone else was doing. Not so much from a place of envy or comparison, but a path of least resistance or following the crowd. If someone seemed like they had it all figured out (which they didn't), I might as well do what they were doing. After all, the freedom of escaping high school meant fun times ahead, right?

As I shared my plans with my parents, they were largely unimpressed. My dad was all for me going to college but told me that working in education wouldn't pay well and why don't I try business? My mom was supportive of what I wanted to do so long as I could earn enough money to support myself. As a woman who married later in life and had a strong nursing career prior to the arrival of her children, my mom understood the importance of education and a career for a woman. To her, it represented independence, self-reliance, and the ability to stand on your own two feet without the need for someone else to support you. Plus, the doors it opened and the knowledge it provided couldn't be taken away. So, while they came from slightly different perspectives, my parents were both excited about the possibility of college for me. What they weren't so on board with was incurring the cost to do it. From their socio-economic porch, college was a win, but not if the literal cost of attending would outweigh the benefit. As a 17-year-old, despite my part-time job and great savings habits, I was largely unaware of what a loan (let alone interest) meant for the long term and I could not get on board with them. I saw college as a haven of fun, exploration, and freedom. Regarding college, I did not share the view from my parents' socio-economic porch. I was more interested in short-term satisfaction than any practical monetary garbage they were spewing.

As the year progressed, our conversations continued. I found myself in our school's career library researching professions and what schools offered what majors. Even then, I had a knack and a love for researching colleges and my time spent there was a time to dream and imagine what was possible for the future. At the end of my search process, I applied to 5 schools. Some public, some private, some larger, and some smaller. All had to have education degrees and they all were in my home state. I received several partial scholarships for which I was both excited and surprised. In the end, though, my parents stood their ground and despite my best efforts to go away, my dreams were thwarted by logic and economics.

After high school graduation, I enrolled in the local community college. I was awarded nearly a full-ride scholarship and with the money I'd already saved from my part-time job, it gave me a great head start on paying for the rest of college. (I should probably mention that my parents had five kids and for college, we were squarely on our own.) Now by today's standards, what my parents subjected me to might be considered harsh or even abusive. If your child has good grades and the desire to go away to college, shouldn't you oblige them? My parents weren't like anyone else's, though, and the verdict stood. And you know what? It worked out. I was pretty darn happy in retrospect. I liked my classes, my peers, and my professors. I was inducted into the honor society on campus which opened a few more doors, and I took advantage of other hands-on learning opportunities and lectures they had on campus. I ended up with one awesome advisor who helped me tremendously. She not only believed in me, but she also helped me navigate getting my degree so I could transfer to a four-year school when my two years were up. She even encouraged me to apply for a transfer scholarship. I have every confidence she was a game-changer for me. I also discovered that I was a bit of a homebody (more so than I thought). Living at home in college had different rules than those I had in high school, and I enjoyed the new-found freedom of running my own life.

So off I went—college by day and working by evenings and weekends. I kept my part-time job for which I'd received a promotion and pay increase. During my time at the community college, I carried 15-17 credit hours each semester and worked an average of 30 hours per week. It wasn't easy, but I fell into a routine by which I learned to multi-task, prioritize, and run my own life. I saved my money for the next two years and kept my grades up to keep my scholarship. As my first two years of college were winding down, I was confident I was ready to fly the coop for the last two years and move out of the house. But then life had other plans and I had to readjust my sails yet again.

If you've ever seen the movie "It's a Wonderful Life" repeatedly like I have, then you are familiar with the life of George Bailey. The young man who aspires to shake the dust of the small town of Bedford Falls from his feet and go off to college and see the world. You will also remember that other factors intruded on his plans—a war, the death of his father, and the exit of his younger brother, Harry, who leaves town to work for his father-in-law. Every time George Bailey tried to escape, life reeled him back in to stay in Bedford Falls. My life's story is not much different than George Bailey's.

Shortly after I had graduated high school, my mother was diagnosed with cancer later that summer. It was out of left field. It was a bit of uncertainty, but my mom played it off as beatable. The doctors described her surgery as 'successful' and for this kid of 18 years, I took them at their word. The next couple of years rolled along okay. My parents took some trips and enjoyed life. I continued with school and working. Again, that familiar routine hummed along.

But near the time I was planning my escape for the next two years of college, I knew something was wrong. My mom seemed more fatigued, often sleeping long hours and looking worn. I tried to ignore it, but my gut told me something was off. While I had already decided to attend college locally or within two hours, I had already decided to move to the dorms. I wanted my freedom and I was ready! But, as the months passed, my gut told me to keep my part-time job, enroll locally, and commute. This was not what I wanted. But I enrolled in a small liberal arts college about 20 miles from home (who had given me the best scholarship of the two schools I'd applied to) and made the commute each day all while continuing to work. The commute was a heavily traveled route and was eating up a lot of time in my days. School was new and there was a learning curve there. I had gotten a good education at the community college, and I could handle the rigor at the new school. It was learning the new routines, campus, professors, and resources that took that first semester to get on my feet. But I was determined and wanted my degree in four years. As my mom got sicker following her second surgery, the workload at home besides work and school felt heavier too. While they never imposed "must do's" upon me, I helped with more major responsibilities around the house—the grocery shopping, laundry, and Christmas shopping for the family's gifts that my mom didn't feel up to doing led the list followed quickly by wrapping said gifts. My life was a busy whirlwind of activity most of the time and the time passed quickly those two years.

After two years, I applied for graduation. I graduated with a bachelor's degree in business administration. (Somewhere along the line I'd decided teaching elementary school wasn't for me.) When graduation came around that May, my mom was there along with the rest of my family to hear my name called and watch me walk across the stage. I had no idea how I got there. It all seemed a blur, yet it all seemed worth it too. My mom died 8 months later.

After working for a year in my first 'real' job (and hating it), I returned to my roots of wanting to go into education. I was working two jobs at the time—my 'real' job as well as the job I had in college. I let go of the real job and kept the part-time job while I applied to graduate school for their counseling program. Paying for it would be quite a challenge. I'd managed between scholarships, commuting, and working to pay for undergrad without a loan. But grad school was a different animal. The cost per credit hour was enormous by comparison. I knew if I could get hired by the local university, they would pay 75% of my master's program after I worked there for six months. I applied for employment several months before enrolling in the counseling program and nothing. Then there was that moment of saving grace when a neighbor working at the university informed me someone in her office had quit. She helped me get an interview in the Athletics Department at the university working as a secretary. Not an impressive job for someone with a bachelor's degree, but I didn't care. I took the job. The pay was horrible. I could barely make rent, as I was living on my own by then, but the upshot was huge tuition savings and that was enough for me. For the next two and a half years, it was work by day and full-time grad school by night. After graduation, I took a job as a high school counselor in a rural community an hour away. It paid horribly, but because I had no debt from grad school either, I could pay the bills and finally live on my own with no roommate necessary. My career found its way from there and while I still worked part-time jobs to supplement my educator pay, things slowly got more comfortable as the years rolled by. The rest, as they say, is history.

So why tell you my story? It surely does not impress from an educational standpoint. There was no 'dream' school or 'name brand' school. There are no tales of sorority dances or travel abroad. There was no leaving home at 18 to find myself or immerse myself in a college that would leave me with great memories on my road to adulthood. Rather, my story is pretty 'blah' and some might think, if possible, one to be avoided! I went back and forth on whether to even put the story of my own college experience in this book. I must admit I don't share my story much with others and writing it down was much more emotional than I thought to re-live those dark times. I included my story in this book because I didn't want you to think I had some pie-in-the-sky "utopian" college experience. I wanted you to hear that there are a lot of ways to get your college degree, but the road might not always be easy or pretty. I wanted to be a living example of how you too can have a life that's a hot mess and still wind up okay in the end.

My story is typical of millions of people who have worked lots of jobs and worked hard to piece together an education they wanted for themselves. My story isn't even that bad. It's probably typical for all I know. There are stories every year around gradu-ation time about obstacles overcome and hardships taken on by people who want more for their life. Those with the tenacity to stick with it even when the going got tough. My path had its blessings despite the rough patches. I never lived in my car or chose a path of unsurmountable student loan debt that crippled my life after graduation. I wasn't a single mom trying to make it through. I had no learning challenges or other obstacles to overcome. Had I been someone more financially blessed, though, my story would have been different. Had I been someone without personal extenuating circumstances like a parent with cancer or who wasn't (as it turned out) a homebody then perhaps the story I just told you would have had quite a different narrative. The decisions I made regarding my honeycomb might have looked differently had I had different circumstances. Perhaps I'd put less emphasis on the financial piece or more on the academics had I felt those were stronger considerations. But, for me, my *whys* of choosing how to pursue my college education put more emphasis on finances and less on the social piece. Had I been dealt different cards; I might have had a different life altogether.

I will not deny there were downsides to my choices. Some sacrifices were made and there were jealous moments along the way as I watched friends enjoy other options. I missed out on experiences others had but given the choice to either not go to college at all or do it the way I did, I would choose the route I took all over again. Sure, I may have had to live vicariously through others occasionally. But it was a short span of my life and it worked out great for me in the long term. And what better job could I have than helping other people improve the quality of their lives through education and seeing what great adventures await them even if I didn't have the same opportunities or experiences?

But the fact is, it is what it is. There are rare times when I hear from one of my students who shares a tale from college—traveling abroad, internships in new cities, off-campus apartments, and making great plans—that I get a little wistful. I think of what might have been had the opportunities laid before me been different. Then I realize this student will have ups and downs in life as well. We all play the cards we are dealt. I just tried to play mine the best I could. I made mistakes and some things probably seem unappealing when thinking of what your college years might look like. But I must say there have been so many positives that have come from my college experience that would never have been possible had I done it any other way. Had I done what the lopsided honeycomb I had constructed for myself entailed I would have focused way too much on the social side of things. I would have ignored the financial side completely. My emotional side would never have been fed properly and, I doubt I would've been able to enjoy myself away at school always wondering (and worrying) what was going on at home with my mom. The benefits of my bizarre, off-kilter college experience? There were many.

I learned a work ethic I know I would never have possessed had it not been for the challenges presented by commuting and living at home. Working and going to school helped me learn to be more responsible, multi-task, and juggle multiple projects and deadlines at once. Living at home, while difficult, gave me time with my mom I would not have had otherwise. I cherish those late-night conversations we had after I got home from work. A lot of wisdom was imparted in those talks. Had I gone away to school I wouldn't have those memories. It was a trade-off, but one that was worth it in hindsight.

I also found a core group of friends despite not being away at school. These were my people. I'd found them at work, in the classroom, in the cafeteria. They lived a life a lot like mine—not a lot of money, juggling jobs with school and family commitments. Like me, they wanted life to be different at times, but they played the cards they were dealt, and they played them well. Today, they are established and successful on every level. Many of these people I still count among my greatest friends. I eventually married one of those great friends. Had my college path been different, I doubt we'd ever met.

The point of all this is to drive home the reality that there are a million ways to get an education after high school. **I'm not sure it matters so much where you go—trade school, community college, or 4-year college or if you enter the military as it does that you are moving forward and improving yourself.** For most of us, college is not necessarily glamorous, easy or even fun. And if anyone feeds you a line that 'college is the best four years of your life', just walk away. If someone told me back then college was the best four years of my life, I would have been so depressed. From my perspective, I had nowhere to go but up.

The best way to move yourself up in life is to get additional training. We need that training to separate ourselves from the crowd. A high school diploma on its own doesn't get you too far these days. You must have something from a training stand-point that cannot be taken away from you—a trade, a degree, a skill set—something that utilizes and maximizes your talents you can contribute to the workforce. What's important in finding that right path, though, is taking a thorough look at all the factors that contribute to your success in college and putting together a plan that provides you some stability and makes you as strong and resilient as you can be at this age. Just like the honeycomb with its hexagon design, what factors will make you strongest to take on the educational and/or training path to get where you want to go?

Academics

The college scam story that broke in the Spring of 2019 floored many of us. Whether you were a parent, a student, or worked in the industry like me, the boldness (and audacity) of the plan that had unfolded was shocking. If you aren't familiar with the story, there were several families from across the country (including some predominant movie stars) who paid people to take their kids' college entrance exams or get them admitted to college under the auspice of being an athlete for a sport they did not even play. Still others made large 'donations' to faux charities in exchange for admission favors all while lining the pockets of some very crooked people. While most people's reaction to this story was one of shock or even anger, I had a quite different reaction. My first reaction was one of pity. Pity for the children of these parents. My first thought was, "How sad is it for this child that his/her parents think he/she is so stupid that they must do it for them"? The message these parents sent their nearly adult children was that they had come up short, they weren't enough, they couldn't make it on their own, they were a failure as a human. The message they sent said they didn't believe in their kid. How sad is that? Nothing is more heartbreaking for a child than to disappoint their parents. Kids make mistakes as we all do. Maturity comes at different times. Just because a student isn't a good tester or doesn't care for school, doesn't mean they're a screw-up or incapable of succeeding. What a horrible and damaging message these parents sent their kids. For some, I imagine the damage done by this one act of cheating has sent a message so powerful to these teens that the relationship between their parents and them may be irretrievably broken or, at the very least, strained and fragile. And damaged or broken relationships between a parent and a child are way more heartbreaking than not getting into a good school. I'm positive these parents had good intentions. I don't know if those intentions were to protect and/or help their child or to boost their own egos. Regardless, I am confident that the motivator for this behavior was, on some level, fueled by status.

As I mentioned in the foreword, working in college counseling has given me a front-row view on the college admission process. It is, at times, a voyeuristic view of how people think and act when posed with different situations. Sometimes it is moving and inspirational and, at others, it is jaw-dropping and disappointing. Perhaps the most disappointing aspect of the college process is the hang-ups that people have about the 'status' of the college. I will not deny that some schools are academically stronger than others. We all know that. What's disturbing is that sometimes a person's WORTH and potential for success in life is judged based on where they have gone to college. What's happened to our worth as a person being enough just by our existing? Of course, we all have the capacity for improvement and education is one segue to improving ourselves. However, I have seen smart kids drink their way out of an elite institution and seen below-average students who attend a 'lesser' school rise to the challenge and thrive in college and the real world. **Let's not confuse status with character.** Who you are has nothing to do with where you go and who you will become is up to you and your own decisions and actions.

A few years back I had the opportunity to tour a college on the east coast. As part of our experience at the college, they paired the visiting counselors with faculty from various departments for a Q&A session. The faculty panel I attended included two super nice professors from the chemistry department who worked with the graduate students. One of the visiting counselors asked them if it mattered in the graduate admission process where the students had done their undergraduate work. The one professor seemed a little puzzled by the question but answered it anyway. In essence, he said that it didn't matter to them where the student had gone to undergraduate school so much as it mattered that they did their best there, that they were at or near the top of the class at their chosen school, and had done research or made other contributions to the field of chemistry. They were looking for students who were accomplished but teachable and wanted to learn. After he answered the question, he asked the woman why she wanted to know that. She explained to them she had a lot of pressure from parents at her school that their son or daughter be at "the best" college or university as an undergraduate to secure top billing for graduate school. The professor smiled and responded that his students came from all over and then named the schools. I must admit some were pretty mainstream (and some I'd never even heard of), but when he spoke of their accomplishments and the research they were doing at the graduate level, I had no doubt those students had chosen their undergraduate institutions wisely. They had done their homework and listened to what school fit their needs. The academic portion of their honeycomb was configured wisely and now they were reaping the benefits. It didn't matter what someone else might deem an 'average' college. What mattered is how they spent their time while they were there. The hard work they'd done at the undergraduate level paid off and now they were stepping up to even bigger things.

I'm not sure why we ever got started on the whole college name thing at all. Remember that presentation I talked about at the beginning of the book? The one where the parents were shocked by what stresses their kids were under? One detail I shared with them during that presentation was statistics on admission to Harvard as an undergraduate. I'll spare you the numbers here, but by my math the numbers of U.S. high school student who go to Harvard when you look at all the details—number of graduating high school seniors, the number who go to college, the number who apply to a four year college, the number who apply to Harvard, the number of students Harvard accepts, the number of students Harvard admits who are from other countries, etc. and you break it all down—the number of people who go to Harvard is minuscule. I'd have to check my notes, but it was something crazy like .000847% of all graduating U.S. seniors go to Harvard. Additionally, my math worked out to .0067% of all graduating U.S. seniors attend an Ivy League in any given year. (And don't start the argument that if they didn't accept international students the number would be higher. Trust me, it wouldn't be that much higher.) I realize my math might be a bit simplified, but the message is this: If so few people go to Harvard, why are we so hung up about using it as a benchmark for college success? I'm not trying to diss Harvard. They do some great stuff, but I think even Harvard hopes their applicants find Harvard is a FIT for them. If not, their academic and personal experiences may suffer. Look beyond the Ivy League schools for just a moment and be honest—how many of us know where our primary care doctors went to medical school? Undergrad? I do only because she knows what I do for a living and it came up in conversation during my office visit. Mostly, we don't know, and it doesn't matter so long as they can do their job and do it well.

Now, nothing is wrong with striving for the best college possible. Not in the least. I wholeheartedly encourage it. The fall of senior year is the time to apply and see where your efforts take you. The key is to find balance. Apply not only to your dream school, but to a core group of schools that will serve you well and are within reach academically, financially, and in other ways. This way, whatever happens in the end, you are covered and have put yourself in a win-win situation. Everyone's dream school is different for them. If during the college application process, you don't try for your dream school, you might wonder 'what if' or miss out on a great opportunity.

A young woman I know shared with me that when she was in high school, her dream school was Brown University. When I asked her why she didn't have a definite answer. She just liked the sound of it and was intrigued by what she learned about the school when she researched it. She knew deep down she was a homebody and she was sure Brown didn't fit her geographic *why* so she let it go. She took the logical route and applied to and enrolled in a college that wound up being a perfect fit for her in her life. She had a successful run there and no regrets about where she attended. Coincidentally, she recently re-enrolled there to get her Ph.D. What she did regret was that she'll never know if she could've gotten into Brown. She missed her window of opportunity just to see what happened. Had she applied, she would have known for sure if she was Brown material or not. Now, she is left wondering about the 'what ifs.' Had she tried for admission and made it in, would she have found the courage to go? Would it have changed the course of her education, her career, her life? Maybe. Maybe not.

Now is the time to dream and pursue what you want. **What you need to dig deep to find, though, is your *why*.** Why do you want to go here? Is it because it fits you on so many levels and checks a lot on your wish list? Or, is it because it will sound good when they call your name at your high school graduation and announce where you will go to college next year? Is it because family members or friends will think better of you (or so you think) if you attend School X? If your why is based on what others think or how you think it makes you look, it's a bad reason. Here's a tip: Step away from your ego. What looks good isn't always what IS good. And the message students are getting is that they must be admitted everywhere and succeed at everything (again, no failure, of course) to be worthy. What a hot mess that idea is.

I will never forget the admission rep who worked at a highly elite college and shared with me (anonymously, of course) a call she had received from a parent that deeply upset her. One day she got a call from a parent who was furious her son was not admitted to the institution where she worked as the admissions director. As most people who've been rejected want to know, the question was *why* her son not admitted. (Now, remember that it's difficult for most admission counselors to answer this question. Truth be told, the admission industry is tricky. Sometimes there are so many qualified candidates that, in some cases, there is not always a clear-cut reason the student wasn't admitted. It's often that sheer numbers prohibit everyone from being accepted and it's sometimes like splitting hairs their qualifications are so close. When someone calls and asks *why*, it's often not a simple, quantitative response. In short: why your kid didn't get accepted is not personal. It's just numbers. And while that may be disappointing, knowing *why* probably wouldn't make you feel better anyway. If anything, accepting the 'no' as simply more information that will move the student to their 'yes' and where they ultimately will be most successful is a good thing to do. If you're a mature, normal adult then you know rejection is a fact of life. We don't always get the guy/girl, the job, the account, whatever. It's just the way the ball bounces. It's not personal. It's just life.)

Meanwhile, back at the ranch...this mom continued to berate the admission counselor and insisted on knowing *why* her son was not admitted. (Just a tip: Berating or threatening an admission rep will never turn out an admission decision from a no to a yes. If anything, you are just making yourself look bad. It's kind of like hanging onto the ankles of someone who broke up with you as they try to walk away.) The admission counselor remained calm and professional and patiently explained what she could. After several minutes of ranting, the mother expressed anger that of the 10 colleges to which her son applied, this one was the only one that had 'rejected' him. The admission counselor was taken aback by this statement. She turned the tables on the mother and confronted her with the real issue as she saw it. She asked where the son was at that moment. The mother responded that he was in the next room. The admission rep wisely responded, "Your son is within earshot in the next room. You tell me he's been accepted to 9 of the 10 institutions to which he has applied. You've named them off and I know they are quite respectable and difficult universities, yet you insist on banging on this one closed door. What message are you sending to your child? Essentially you are telling him he failed because he didn't get into all 10—only 9." With that, the mother finally took a breath and stepped back from the situation. She realized that in her effort to be an advocate for her child and make all things right, she inadvertently sent a strong message to him that he had failed miserably. The admission rep went on further to the mother asking her to instead celebrate the joy of her son having 9 magnificent schools from which to choose and to go tell him how proud she was of HIM and his accomplishments. Shortly after, their call ended and while we will never know where that young man enrolled in college, I can only assume he's thriving at his institution of choice and doing just fine.

A lot of ego is tied up in the academic portion of the college choice. And perhaps, next to financial considerations, the academic side of the hexagon is probably where most families put the weight of their college decision. It makes sense. If you're there to learn, you must be careful not to overshoot or undershoot your education. Much like the *why* you want to go to the Ivy League or school with great name recognition. If it's just for the sake of impressing others or because you think it gives you a guarantee to a great future, you're probably looking at this all wrong.

Academic fit differs from academic reputation. Academic reputation is usually the 'name brand' of colleges and universities. These are the schools that, when we hear their name, we associate with a 'good school.' These are the ones that perhaps invoke thoughts of student intelligence, seasoned professors, and gorgeous campuses. While those are all lovely characteristics of a great academic institution, academic *fit* is far more important.

With over 5000 institutions of higher learning in the U.S., there are plenty of schools from which to choose. This can be overwhelming. With so many schools to choose from, how do we choose one that is the right *fit* academically? Logically, we start with name recognition. It's the school we know because it is one everyone's heard of or gets lots of attention. It seems familiar somehow, so it must be good. And, it probably is. But, is it a good fit for *you?* When we look at academic fit, there is much more than a school's reputation to consider. It is common for me to see students trying to over-shoot the academic portion of their college search because it looks good. Students today have been convinced they must get perfect grades (straight A's) and perfect or near-perfect test scores to get into college. Anything less will leave them behind no future in sight; kicked to the curb with no possibility for redemption. Checking off the boxes for admission seems to be the end game with no thought to the real reason we go to school at all—to learn. Finding academic fit means many things besides just name recognition. It also includes:

- Institutions with programs that fit your interests and potential majors.
- Institutions that allow you to do undergraduate research or other things to 'get your hands dirty' and delve into your major and/or profession.
- Professors that are dedicated, promote class discussion and have a passion for what they do.
- Professors that are approachable, accessible outside of class, mentors, and interested in helping students learn.
- Professors that encourage students to ask questions and make mistakes to further enhance their learning.
- Internships, co-ops, and other opportunities that provide students with academic experiences in the real world.
- On-campus simulation that presents you the opportunity to learn with practical application—simulated stock exchange floors, electronic patients/dummies, research labs,

on-campus radio and tv facilities, etc. Anything that gives you that real-world feel for your major to enhance your learning is a plus.

- Off-campus experiences that will give you a more global perspective or get you outside your comfort zone.
  Things like study abroad or volunteer opportunities (local or global).

- Students that contribute to classroom discussion, aren't afraid to ask questions, are there to learn and not just in it for the grade.

- A place where everyone (faculty, staff, students) has a sense of contributing and lifting up others —not just a place of competition and ego-centric attitudes.

- A balanced approach to learning for YOU—Rigorous, but not so much that it causes constant stress that you're in over your head and constantly trying to keep up. But, not so easy that you are bored, under-challenged, and not reaching your full academic capability.

- Support for any academic area you may need it—writing or math centers, tutors, etc.

- Support for any learning differences you may have including 504 plans and Americans With Disabilities accommodations.

- Supports learning in how you learn best—class discussion, oral and written presentations, hands-on experiences, 1:1 learning, small group work, projects, or a hybrid of all.

- Facilities that support your learning—good library exchange programs, computer labs, etc.

- Learning for the sake of learning. In other words,
  a place that encourages you to be a lifelong learner.

While you may not necessarily need all the characteristics listed above to find your academic fit, you must find which of these are crucial to your future learning. It can take some introspection and self-awareness to determine what you need academically from a college. A student who is determined to find what fits them as an individual will eventually find what they are seeking if they are willing to do the hard work or admitting they need support to succeed.

In one of my college planning sessions, I met with a family whose child was about to embark on the college process. In our discussion, we talked about what they were seeking in a college as well as a conversation on 'return on investment' and I spoke about looking for opportunities at a college or university that would allow the student to grow in terms of employability. I spoke about higher education and the doors it would open. I assumed that what the student wanted their college education to yield was, in fact, a job. You've read my life story. I think it's safe to say I believe education is key to getting a job. I would also hear this repeatedly from families who sat before me discussing their child's academic future: the goal was admission to a good school with a good scholarship followed by a good job. I mistakenly assumed this family felt the same way. Let's just say the dad leveled me and put me in my place. And while he wasn't particularly polite about it, he was right. Who was I to assume that the goal for their child's education was to get a job at the end of their time there? He informed me that their purpose for their child's higher education experience was to find a place intellectually stimulating and encourage the student to be the best version of themselves possible. The goal, as he put it, was learning for the sake of learning. Undoubtedly, he put me in my place. And I deserved it. It wasn't my place to assume what someone else needed—what their *why* was for choosing a college. I'm usually pretty good about standing back and listening and not assuming things, but I had jumped the gun on this one. Even if I did think that education was a means to an employable end, it wasn't fair for me to assume that student had the same perspective or goal as I did. While it stung at the time, in hindsight, I did appreciate that he spoke his mind. It was a humble reminder of my place in this process. Even though I would normally not put myself in that place of assuming I knew what was best, for some reason that day I felt the need to generalize or get ahead of myself in the conversation. Perhaps it was Friday and I was tired or maybe I just had heard the same wish from everyone else that week. Either way, it was a great reminder that I don't know your *why* until you tell me.

Every student approaches the college process differently and that's what makes the job challenging and fun for me. As much as the student I just mentioned wanted a school for the sake of learning, other students might look at college as a status symbol, a trophy, an entitlement. If this is the student's academic *why* then so be it. It's not uncommon for me to see students approach their learning as a series of checkboxes. For these students, they will not likely take a holistic view of academics when selecting a college and will just seek academic reputation over fit. For them, education has been a series of checkboxes—Do the work. Check. Get an A. Check. No confrontation or strife. Check. In other words, they are on the assembly line of learning. A simple A plus B equals C equation. In their minds, education is a linear and smooth experience free of questions, roadblocks, or frustration. From this experience, then, it is logical that their college experience follows the same path: Get good grades. Check. Get high test scores. Check. Be admitted to every college. Check. While this may appear logical, true learning is often not a linear path. Over the years, my students who have been the most prepared for college have had some strife, some academic obstacles or challenges that were not easy. Instead of breaking them or defining them, though, they used it as a springboard to rise to the challenge and overcome it. By my observation, these students were more confident, self-assured, and more likely to advocate for themselves. Even those who thought they couldn't learn something eventually figured it out and gained a lot of self-respect and confidence as opposed to those who claimed their now 'curved' linear path was somehow 'not fair.' Those who fared even worse? Those whose parents intervened and tried to fix it all. By doing that, they did not allow for the natural progression of problem-solving to take place (which, by the way, is also a great form of learning). Sometimes the "B" in a class that presents challenges is better than the easy "A" for aiding students' learning. In the many conversations I've had with hundreds of admission reps over the years, many have said they are sometimes leery of the straight-A student and, instead, feel more comfortable with the B student. Their reasons for this are because the B student often has had struggles or had to make the effort that didn't result in an A in the class and yet they seem to handle adversity or direction better than those with 'perfect' grades. They felt they were more teachable and tended to self-advocate and take more responsibility for their learning. **Even being perfect isn't perfect because sometimes imperfections have their upshots.**

So the bottom line when looking at the academic portion of your college honeycomb is this: look for the school that presents learning opportunities to you in various forms, has the human component that will allow and encourage you to learn, be inquisitive, and develop your own talents all while supporting you as a learner, and will challenge you in appropriate ways with good balance neither under-shooting or over-shooting your abilities. Let go of the name recognition. While a big-name school may be the perfect fit for you, another gem of a school may mold you into who you want to become intellectually. Understand that if you needed academic support in high school for a learning disability such as ADHD, you will need to continue that support in college. **ADHD doesn't go away when they hand you your diploma.** Look at the academic piece in the context of what fits you and not just what everyone else is doing will have the first side of your college honeycomb firmly in place.

Questions to Ask Yourself About Academic Fit

- What scenarios do I value when learning—class discussion, projects, 1:1, etc.

- How do I learn best?

- Do I have diagnosed learning disabilities or other diagnoses related to education?

- Did I receive accommodations or support services for learning disabilities or other situations in high school? If so, is it likely I will need to continue those in college to be successful?

- What kind of student am I? Motivated? Needs support? Important for others to know me?

- Can I handle being 'lost in the crowd' and still be a responsible learner?

- Do I self-advocate well?

- Will the school(s) I am considering allow me to grow—to not be over or under-challenged?

- What opportunities must be available to help me learn? (Internships, hands-on experiences, research opportunities, etc.)

- How does the faculty at the college I am considering assist students with their learning?

- Does the faculty have office hours for me to meet with them if I need help? Does the faculty give out their email address or cell phone number in case I need to reach them with questions? How accessible is the faculty at the college I am considering?

- Will a teacher's aide be teaching my course or a professor?

Financial

The second portion of the honeycomb is financial. As you can imagine, in addition to the academic considerations, finances are a huge factor in the college decision process. Even though parents and grandparents may have saved and saved for their loved one's college tuition since birth, it's very common to come up short. The pace at which college tuition costs are rising has outpaced inflation for several years and it's taking its toll. Much like the housing boom that eventually collapsed as people over-borrowed for more house than they could afford, the same is happening with college. Student loans are skyrocketing and the default rate (those not paying on their student loans) is at an all-time high. High debt that outpaces entry-level wages is causing people to walk away from their student loans and at quite a price. Unlike a mortgage where you can throw the keys in the mailbox and drive away, student loan debt will follow you to the grave. And, if you are a parent who wants to help their child by co-signing a student loan, beware! If you co-sign a loan for your child and the child defaults, then you are stuck with the bill. It may not seem like a big deal, but if you are not financially viable, run into health issues, or are nearing retirement, the burden of a student loan can quickly deplete any reserves you had set aside for yourself.

People can get nasty about money too. What's that saying? Don't talk about religion, money, or politics? I've seen people say and do some nasty stuff regarding money over the years and make themselves look like a jerk rather than accept their financial limitations and the financial restraints the college may have. While I have heard some pretty pathetic stories of parents behaving badly, one story about a parent who cornered an admission rep at a high school event sticks in my mind.

In general, college admission reps are some of the nicest, most helpful people I have ever met working in education. Their hearts are in the right spot, they cheer on and hope for their potential students, and they want to see students succeed. They are hard-working and resourceful. What they are not are paid well. Their work hours are crazy—sometimes visiting schools by day and doing college fairs or high school presentations by night. The fall is especially grueling. Despite the long days during the week, they might also have college fairs or travel on the weekends. All this PLUS they read your essays, respond to your emails and answer your calls. It's a lot to juggle.

That is why I found one story of a rep berated by a parent after a college night particularly upsetting. The rep had just made the five-hour drive from out of state leaving well before dawn, spent the rest of the day visiting various high schools in the area and meeting with students. After that, he headed to a college night where he gave a full presentation he was requested to do by the school. On his way to the car—well after 9 pm—he was cornered in the parking lot by a parent who 'wanted a minute of his time.' The rep obliged only to be subjected to an onslaught of put-downs and 'piece of mind' discussion (albeit one-sided) about how his son was not given a fair financial aid package at this rep's institution the previous year and the dad subsequently sent the son to a school that was able to provide the needed award package. The rep apologized for the school's inability to do more, explained the limitations of their endowments and scholarship resources all to no avail. The onslaught continued for nearly 20 minutes. As if the verbal lashing wasn't enough, the admission rep reported that when the parent was done, he walked away, got into his fancy car and drove off. The rep, in turn, got in his rental car, exhausted, and headed for the hotel to check-in.

Had the parent considered for a moment he could have any responsibility in this? Could he have chosen a more affordable option on the son's list of schools? Might he have had a better conversation with someone in the financial aid office when this happened—and not a year later? Could he have admitted a school was financially out of reach rather than push the boundaries beyond the ways the school could support him? These reps are people. Not machines, not monsters. People. When choosing the financial side of your honeycomb, ask yourself this: Is this my issue or theirs? It's usually ours. We decide which schools are financially doable and within reach—with or without aid. Don't back yourself into a corner and limit yourself to pricey, out-of-range schools only. Again, it's good to dream. But the numbers must add up. Perhaps that father felt he was a failure to his son—that he'd come up short and didn't want to admit there simply wasn't enough in the coffers to make it work at this school. I'm confident he was feeling frustrated and I get that. I don't get why he had to make it personal with someone who had little or no control over the outcome based on decisions this family made. I'm glad his son wasn't there to witness this outburst.

Had this family spent more time examining the financial side of their honeycomb, this confrontation could have been avoided.

One purpose of education is to build oneself up—to possess knowledge, training, a skillset; to provide a better quality of life and greater income. These things are all true, however, they come at a price. **Education, when its costs surpass its benefits, becomes a burden rather than a segue to a better quality of life.** For years, society has been selling the hype of education as a ticket out—a ticket out of poverty, worry, shame, ignorance—and we as consumers have been buying what they're selling. But one must consider the larger ramification of the cost of the education. Education is still a ticket out of all those things, BUT one must leverage the cost of education against what the payoffs will be. In theory, it would be great if we could all afford that $70,000 per year institution because it promised to provide the most stellar education available and guaranteed six-figure incomes after graduation and no chance of layoffs. But realistically, most of us fall to the middle or the bottom of the pack from a financial standpoint. That's depressing, but there is good news. Not every school is $70,000 per year and, while still expensive, many schools offer good bang for their buck. The job of a parent (and the student) is to work to find post-secondary options that cover a wide gamut of price ranges. Let me give you an example:

Let's say a student wants to major in Physical Therapy. They might be willing to stay in their home state but have their eye on a pricey, private institution that costs $65,000 per year. They also know their in-state public flagship university also has a Physical Therapy program and they can attend there for less than $25,000 per year. If this student was concerned with name only and getting 'the best' education in terms of reputation, they might fill their list of potential colleges to apply to with other private institutions in that $65,000 range from all around the country and leave the less expensive state institutions off the application list. They know what they want, why not just go for it all? What's the problem with this, you ask? The problem is you can't put all your eggs in one basket.

There are a lot of unknowns in life. And expenses that pop up are no exception. Many people I have worked with have assumed (often incorrectly) that they will qualify for financial aid that will not need to be repaid or get a big scholarship because they have good grades and test scores or attended a certain high school. Others have an "I'll worry about it later" mentality. Still others believe, "I'll have a good job and pay it off after the fact." But sometimes, those ships don't come in.

Early in my career, I worked with a young woman on my counseling load who came from recently divorced parents. The oldest of several children, she was confident her single, lower-income dad with whom she resided would make her eligible for government financial aid. With that mindset, she pressed on to apply to a multitude of high-end, expensive schools. While academically I was not concerned about her ability to be admitted, I was concerned about her ability to pay for these schools. I shared my concerns with her, and she assured me she had this under control. She applied diligently and on time to all big-name institutions and completed their scholarship applications. Nowhere on her list was a single in-state public institution or any institution known for giving large scholarships or aid to someone of her caliber. Every school was top-notch in her mind—stellar in academics and aesthetics and name recognition. The problem was all her eggs were in one financial basket. Most people don't pay the 'sticker price' for their education. There is usually SOME aid or SOME scholarship awarded but given the big price tag, it often can't make a big enough dent in the bottom line to make it financially viable for the student without incurring some big-time pocket-digging or loan-signing. With all her eggs in one financial basket, I feared that the schools wouldn't deliver a suitable financial aid package and she had no back-up plan. And, unfortunately, I was right. She had been admitted to several schools, but no financial resources offered to her could make it feasible for her to go. And, because she'd missed the application and scholarship deadlines for the other schools that would have been viable options, she was now looking at the possibility of not being able to still be admitted at that late date. Beyond that, she no longer qualified for scholarships or financial aid because she missed those deadlines. In the end? She scrambled (after many arguments at home) and enrolled herself in a community college out of state next to her dream school with hopes to one day transfer there. I have no idea what happened to her. I am confident she landed on her feet. She was just that kind of person. But I wish she would've spared herself the pain of having all her financial eggs in one basket.

I've also seen students' due diligence be a game-changer in where they choose to attend school. By applying to a variety of scholarships, one student came up big when she won a $10,000 private scholarship she could use at the school of her choice. Her parents had 5 or 6 kids and she was one of the older ones. Because of this, they made their financial limitations for their children well known and the student was expected to incur loans for the difference although the parents discouraged that. They wanted their children to start their adult life with as little debt as possible so they would not be saddled with extra expenses and start their life 'in the red.' Knowing how her parents felt about debt, the student had her sights on two major universities—a highly respected state university that she liked a great deal and a pricier 'dream' school that was a bit out of reach financially. The student was more than okay with the first school, but after winning the $10,000 scholarship, and with other financial aid, the student's dream school was squarely in reach and she went for it. Her parents supported her 100% and were proud of her effort in going the extra mile.

But whether it's a student having good intentions and falling short financially or the student who follows through on every financial opportunity to find it pay off big, the saddest financial situation is when someone apologizes for their inability to do more for their child. I distinctly remember a situation when a family I was working with came to me so we could meet to discuss the student's college plans. No more than greetings were exchanged, the parents blurted out that they were sorry, but the best they could do to provide financially for their student's college education was community college and then probably transfer to a four-year school. Immediately, I stopped them and told them not to apologize for anything! These people had worked SO hard and provided their child with the best life they possibly could. There was absolutely no reason for them to be apologetic or ashamed. I couldn't help but feel that societal stigma or that keeping up with Joneses mentality from others had them feeling like they'd come up short or somehow failed their child. **No parent should ever feel 'less than' because they aren't bottomless pits of money. Money has little to do with raising a quality human being.** These were loving and caring parents and it was reflected in their child. What they had accomplished in raising a great kid spoke volumes over what college the student would attend. After listening to their story, we took a few minutes to talk through everything and then planned a strategy

for community college and how we might best align her for transferring to a four-year university after that. I applauded these parents
for their honesty and vulnerability. By being honest about their
limitations, we could expedite the conversation to talk about what
would work for them financially and come up with a plan that
firmly placed the financial piece of the student's honeycomb as a
solid foundation for her future education. I can only imagine what
financial hardship they might have incurred and what financial
burden they might still carry today had they not had the courage
to say what was the best choice for them.

They say the one constant in life is change and working in the
college counseling field is no exception. I have seen a sharp change
in attitude in the last 10 years from the student who will attend
college at any cost and sees it as an 'investment' to the student of
today who is much more pragmatic about the costs. I am amazed
at the students today telling me they don't want big debt. Yes, they
want an education and the experience, but not at the expense of
their future. These Generation Z students are much savvier about
money than their Millennial predecessors and I can tell they were
raised during the recession. They are leery and even a tad jaded
about college costs. While their pragmatic inclination is good, what
scares me is that I am hearing more people say, "We can't afford
college, so we won't go at all." What scares me about that is the
"all or nothing" attitude. It's kind of like me saying "I can't afford
a car, so I just won't drive." The reality may more likely be I can't
afford a Jaguar, but my Honda is getting me around town just fine.
Why give up driving completely just because you can't afford the
Jaguar? **Adjust your sails to fit your budget.** College is still a great
investment. It's keeping your costs in line with your resources that
make the difference.

So how can you lighten your financial burden for college?
Here are a few suggestions:

- Consider schools with tuition locks. This means the price won't go up from the time you enroll until the time you graduate (four years later). By doing this, you can escape tuition hikes that usually average between three and seven percent annually.
- Pick schools with a wide range of tuition costs. (Community colleges are generally the least expensive.) From there, choose schools with different price points. Don't pick schools with all the same tuition. If you don't qualify for aid at one, you may not qualify for aid at the others. This will leave you very few options in the end. Again, don't put all your financial eggs in one basket.
- Look for scholarships everywhere! Not just from the college or university themselves, but also from private sources that will usually let you use the money at the college of your choice. There are lots of private scholarship search engines online. But never pay for a scholarship search. That defeats the purpose! You shouldn't be spending money to get money.
- Keep those grades and standardized test scores up! Whenever you have good numbers, you can help increase your chances of a scholarship. Higher credentials can correlate with higher dollar amounts in some situations.

Questions to Ask Yourself About Financial Fit

- How much is saved for my education?
  (Divide that out by 4-6 years to get an idea of how much cash you can come up with out-of-pocket each year of college.)

- Do I want to add graduate/medical/law or another professional program after getting a 4-year degree? (This will add to your expenses.)

- Can/am I willing to commute to reduce living (residential life/dorm) expenses?

- How much does it cost to travel from my home to the school I am considering? (Gas, flights, etc.)

- How much debt am I willing (and reasonably able) to take on in loan repayments? (Use an online calculator to determine what the monthly payment would be.)

- How do I envision student loan debt affecting the quality of my life or that of my family's life after graduation?

- Do I have other things I will be financially responsible for (or want to do) after college graduation (Buying a car, living independently, grad school, travel, etc.) that might be affected by student loan debt?

- Do I know what my monthly payment will be if I borrow _____(fill in the blank—10K, 20K, 30K dollars) over the course of my education? (Use an online calculator to determine this BEFORE you decide on a college!)

Geographic

About 10 years ago, I read an article about students and how far they travel to attend college and I was shocked by the answer. In a society where we often equate distance the student travels with the 'success' or 'status' of the student's education, I was amazed at what a short distance the average student in the U.S. travels to college. Would you like to venture a guess? A mere 71 miles from home. That's it! When you consider all those who travel across the country, versus across the state, versus across town, the average was just 71 miles. Now, I have no idea how they arrived at that statistic. But when my students are hung up on going far away and I ask them "why", it often has something to do with it 'looks better' or they just want to escape the familiar bonds of whatever home is. Either way, we have a frank conversation about location and success and how they are mutually exclusive of one another. You don't have to go far geographically to succeed and going far doesn't guarantee you'll succeed or be happy. (The problems we run from find us wherever we go). There are a million reasons to go far or stay near. No one formula that tells you what you must do. What works is to find your *why*.

Over the years, I have heard from hundreds of students and families on their geographical *why* for their college destination. Some of their reasons have been personal, professional, logical, illogical, or climate-driven. But most have been motivated by what works for them and that's a perfect reason. People don't always give much consideration to the location of the college mostly because they don't look at the wider scope of the decision. Yes, most students will stop to consider the college's community setting—urban, college town, rural, etc. They will consider what type of vibe they want the community to have. What some don't consider is the impact the miles (or lack of miles) will have on their college experience. Whether the examples that follow resonate with you or not, it is always a good idea to have a geographic 'back-up' plan. What that generally means is a closer-to-home option if the original plan doesn't work. For example, the student who wants to go halfway across the country (or all the way) should also have a school selected that is closer to home—say maybe a few hours away. The student whose maximum travel distance is four hours might want to have an in-town option.

The reason for a back-up plan geographically is usually for one of three reasons:

1. The cost of the original plan becomes out of reach and travel expenses are too much.

2. The student realizes at the last minute that the leap to the school farthest away is too much and they aren't quite ready for it.

3. Unforeseen events precipitate a school selection closer to home.

While the first two examples are self-explanatory, the unforeseen events are the ones we must address. There are a few major events over the last 25 years that happened on a national level that I saw change the course for some students and where they geographically chose to attend college. The first was event was September 11, 2001. No one could have predicted the events of that day were coming and yet it affected where students applied to or attended school. Because of the unknown factors—we didn't know if more attacks were coming or where they would happen—some families had their children apply to schools in the center of the country away from larger cities on the coast or they had them apply closer to home. People were scared and wanted to be together. Flights were grounded for nearly a week leaving people scrambling for rental cars. Perhaps families saw being in closer proximity as a safer option or they wanted their students to be within driving distance should an emergency arise. I saw within my school's student population that parents who just six months before planned on having their students travel across the country suddenly reverse course and consider closer options. In hindsight, there were no subsequent attacks and flights resumed normal operations. But at the time, the unknown motivated some people's decisions from a geographic standpoint.

The second scenario that affected student's geographic decisions was based on the financial implications of the recession of 2008. In some cases, families had saved for nearly 18 years for their student to attend college. But the stock market plummet and job layoffs that followed were insurmountable for many families. Being realistic after watching their college investments tied to the stock market shrivel up, many families broke the news to their students they simply could not afford to fly them across the country to attend college and they would have to come up with an alternate plan.

As devastating as this may have been for some students, logic and necessity ruled. It affected not only the students who graduated in 2008 and 2009 but had a ripple effect for later classes as families played catch-up or tended to more urgent matters like keeping a roof over their head, food on the table, or finding a job. There was a lot of uncertainty at that time too and we didn't know how long it would last. Again, in retrospect, things turned around eventually, but I know people whose lifestyles are still much more modest than they were 10 years ago as they continue to catch up.

A third event that changed the geographic course for some students was Hurricane Katrina. Because the hurricane happened at the beginning of the college application season, it affected colleges in the area on two levels. The first was for the students already enrolled. Because the infrastructure of New Orleans was so heavily damaged, students already attending college in the New Orleans area were forced to transfer to other institutions in other parts of the U.S. In some cases, those colleges who had other campuses with whom they were affiliated were able to transfer their students for the remainder of the year. SOME students found themselves suddenly attending college in St. Louis, Chicago, or Denver instead of New Orleans. Agreements were made between the colleges to transfer credits back the following fall to their New Orleans' institution. Since the hurricane coincided with the start of school, students were barely unpacked when they were forced to leave. For the freshmen, they barely had the opportunity for their college experience to begin. Some students transferred back to their New Orleans school the following fall as the city began to rebuild while others never returned.

For high school seniors just beginning their college search, Hurricane Katrina affected them differently. For these students, they had to weigh the risk of whether a New Orleans college was a viable option for them to apply to and attend that next fall since no one knew how the rebuilding process would go or if the city would ever recover. For these students, they knew from the beginning they needed a geographic back-up plan. They could apply to a New Orleans college, but they had to have another option if the school would not be open the following fall. While these students had advance notice of this situation, other disasters like tornadoes and earthquakes could also thwart the best-laid plans. And while we cannot predict those (or even worry about them), it's always a good idea to have diversity in your list of colleges from a geographic standpoint.

We can't prepare for those unforeseen events in life: terrorist attacks, stock market crashes, or natural disasters. And while none of the previous examples may happen to you, there are plenty of other 'unknowns' that happen like illnesses, accidents, or the ever-popular 'I changed my mind.' What we can do to lessen the unknown, though, is leave some breathing room by applying to alternate schools geographically closer to home as a 'just in case.' You may not need to go there, but it's a nice safety net if the unpredictable or unforeseeable happens.

For most students their geographical *why* is varied. They choose their geographic location by what pressing need it fills in context to the rest of their lives. It's not uncommon for these to overlap into the Personal portion of the hexagon. As you'll find, the honeycomb connects and touches all sides and sometimes one category influences another. Among the various reasons I have heard students choose a particular school includes the major they are seeking, family matters, or proximity to family just to name a few.

Sometimes a student will choose a college far from home

because of the unique major they've chosen or the proximity to the experience. If you want to major in marine biology, it's a tougher sell in the Midwest than it is living on the California or Florida coastlines. Perhaps you are interested in Hospitality Management and want all-in with the tourist experience. For you, maybe school in Vegas is the way to go. Or, you want to be a trauma nurse and you want to be near a big city where populations are large and the exposure to a variety of experiences can happen. That's not to say you can't get a good education in or near your backyard, but sometimes getting into the best program or proximity to the best experience necessitates a big move. Exposure to new experiences or admission to a top-notch program might be your geographic *why*.

But what if the best program in the country might be in your backyard? Students who want to be at the 'best' school for their major sometimes find that the best program is just a couple hours away or maybe even in town. This can become a conflict if the student wants the best program AND wants to have an out-of-town or out-of-state college experience. For this student, they must find their geographic *why*. This situation can be a tough one—do you choose proximity and sacrifice exposure in a new community so you can have the best program available to you? Or, do you expose yourself to a new community farther from home and take in those experiences and sacrifice the stronger program? That's a tough one. Both options have pluses and minuses. The student must dig deep and find their *why* if they want to find the place they can succeed. This is one situation that requires bravery, vulnerability, and the courage to dig deep and find what's best for them and listen to their inner voice. No one said this would be easy!

One of the most heartwarming reasons a student gave me for wanting to be close to home was family. His mom had just given birth to a child the year before. While he intended on leaving town, going elsewhere for new experiences, and being out on his own, he wanted to be nearby so he could get home to see his little brother grow up. He wanted to be there for birthday parties and holidays and the random 'firsts' he knew his brother would have. He told me he knew that the four years he would be gone would be such a pivotal time of growth for this brother and he didn't want him to not know who he was. By the time he would return from college his younger brother would be in kindergarten. He didn't want his brother to not know who he was because he only saw him a couple of times a year had he traveled across the county. His brother was his geographic *why*.

Other reasons I've seen students choose a college closer to home include those whose family business required them to be in the vicinity so they could help regularly. Others have been self-proclaimed homebodies. Some students like the community in which they live and want to experience it from another vantage point as a college student living independently in a residential hall. Others have part-time jobs they want to keep, want to save money by commuting, or just found what they're looking for in or near their backyard.

Reasons for students to choose a college or university that is geographically distant are varied as well. Besides finding that one right program or majors, others go because their parents and they have decided it will be good for them to experience life in another community, culture, or setting diametric to what they have already experienced. Some choose colleges that are in big cities after being raised in rural areas, some travel from one coast to the other while others opt to choose their college destination based on climate. Again, no one can determine someone else's *why* and if it's a decision that's been well thought out and subject to a thorough discernment process, we have no business weighing in (unless you are the one paying the bill). We are all entitled to our opinions. If we don't want someone raining on our parade and criticizing our choices, we should probably not be weighing in on theirs. It should suffice to say that we are happy for others that they found their fit and we found ours. Jealousy and competition are never complimentary.

The reasons a person chooses their geographic location shouldn't matter to anyone but them and their family. If their geographic location checks off the boxes on their list of *whys* then it doesn't matter what anyone else thinks about where they go to college. I've seen parents draw a big circle on a map and tell a student they must stay within a certain mile radius. I've seen parents put the stamp of approval on a student's destination because they have family in the area that could help the student should an emergency arise, and I've even seen parents agree to let students attend college in any city that Southwest Airlines flies! The bottom line is that whatever your *why* is dictates your free will choice to choose what's best for you.

Many families I have worked with focused on the academic side of the honeycomb but failed to consider the geographic piece or their child's disposition and temperament. For the families who do this, sometimes the student may have been academically equipped to go to a top-notch college but, from a geographic standpoint, they didn't fare well being far from family. Without the support of loved ones, no amount of academic ability would have them thrive away at college if they couldn't rely on nearby support to keep them going. That's not to say some don't have bouts of homesickness or an adjustment period. Some people just don't thrive when removed from their support system. Knowing yourself and what you need is paramount to your success. Relying on one or two sides of the hexagon—such as academics or finances—and not considering other parameters such as location and support systems—might create an undesirable situation that makes it difficult for the student to thrive (or even survive) if their honeycomb isn't firmly in place and all sides considered. Remember, the stronger the foundation before the student goes to college, the better prepared they are to handle the change and responsibility of being a college student.

Questions to Ask Yourself About Geographic Fit

- What's my motivation for staying close or going far?

- How do I work when not supported by family/friends I can be with regularly?

- Am I mature? Responsible? Independent? Able to advocate for myself?

- Does my parent often 'assist' me in day-to-day tasks that I may struggle with performing or completing on my own?

- Can I multi-task and make deadlines solely by my own efforts?

- Do I make good decisions for myself without guidance or input from others?

- Am I a homebody?

- Am I staying close out of fear or avoidance of change?

- Do I equate geographic location (distance from home) with success or freedom? Is that a motivating factor for me to choose a school?

- Am I staying home out of fear when there is a better option for me elsewhere?

- Am I leaving home and going away to college to avoid a personal situation or problem?

- What are the pluses and minuses of staying home versus going far and vice versa?

Social

It's probably fair to say most high school students seeking a good college fit will consider the Social side of the honeycomb. Students view college as a rite of passage, freedom, independence, and a time to be with peers. That may be true, but most students don't take a wide enough scope of the Social side of the hexagon to understand all the implications. There are a lot of angles to consider socially when looking at colleges. Everything from residential life to Greek life to socio-economic dynamics and school/life balance are all parts of the equation when a student is considering a college that will be a good social fit.

When I meet with families some aspect of the social context of choosing a college usually comes up and this is good. Students must find a place where they feel accepted and can connect with others. Students who report back on their college visits often talk about touring the residence halls and if they liked them or not. And while they should be looking at residence halls in the context of connecting with others and feeling at home, many get caught up in the aesthetics or amenities that the residence halls offer. But dorm living is so much more than just the physical space. Residential life should allow you to be socially comfortable. Does space exist where you can gather collectively to study or socialize? Is there a place within the residence hall that you can disconnect from others and get privacy when you need it? Are there quiet times on the floors?

It's become increasingly popular over the past 15 or 20 years that residential designs have moved from the traditional dorm-style—two to a room with community bathrooms—to a suite-style design. When colleges were moving to this design in the late 1990s, I was on a college tour and saw the display room for one of these new 'suite-style' rooms. I asked the college rep what the motivation was for the design change. He told me that part of the reason was that Housing was having such a tough time with roommate change requests. They discovered that because so many students were being raised in homes where they had their own rooms (and, sometimes, bathrooms) that they essentially didn't know how to share, respect boundaries, or work out differences when sharing space with another student. In all fairness, this wasn't the student's fault. If they hadn't been taught to resolve these types of situations or if they'd never been exposed to sharing a room with a sibling, how could we possibly expect them to work things out with a stranger? From this dilemma, it seems the suite-style residential hall was born.

In the suite-style set-up, there are two to four students per suite with each potentially having their own room. The space will likely have one to two bathrooms as well as a living area and possibly a kitchen. It is much more like an apartment than a dorm. While the set-up of this is beautiful and no doubt appealing, there are some trade-offs. This set-up allows for students to have their own space to retreat to study, sleep, or just have alone time, but it also provides an opportunity for isolation. While everyone needs solitude, isolation is not as desirable. I still see some schools with traditional dorms, but

I'm guessing they're a tough sell on the tour. However, I've had many students tell me that while they didn't want the freshman tradition-al-style dorm room, they saw the value of it after the experience. They viewed it as a learning experience with life lessons in working out differences, learning to communicate and compromise. They viewed it as a fond memory and a rite of passage. However, most were always happy to move on to more deluxe accommodations.

You can't blame a student for being drawn to the residential halls as a decision-maker or deal-breaker when choosing a college. College is largely social. Where you live for the next four (or more) years of your life is paramount and much of your social devel-opment at college will happen in the residential halls. This will become home. But if you want to get the most out of your housing experience from a social vantage point, you must widen the scope of how the residential halls can socially help you. To connect students (especially on large campuses), some colleges are playing match-maker—not in the dating sense—but in connecting individuals with similar interests. As an example, some colleges have introduced living-learning communities where they house all the students who are biology majors, for example, together in the same residential hall. This is, of course, is voluntary and students don't have to join a living-learning community, but it gives them a sense of connect-edness with people they already have something in common with (major) and it also gives them proximity to talk, study, and meet.

Other schools group student housing by interest—music, athletics, honors programs. Grouping like-minded people can often help people connect and transition to college easier. While you don't have to stay living in a learning or interest community all four years, it might be a great way to find some common ground and establish friendships for the remaining years on campus. This might be a great segue to creating strong bonds with others and offsetting the homesickness and loneliness many students experience but never talk about with anyone. When you tour campuses, try to get a feel for what the colleges are doing to connect students and make them feel at home.

Many schools have a requirement that students live in the residence halls for the first year of college. They do this to connect students and help keep a watchful eye as they adjust to college life and making adult decisions unsupervised. Key cards, quiet hours, and someone seeing you come and go are some ways that colleges keep an eye on students. Also, keeping students on campus is another way they can make sure they go to class and have meals provided. But, after that first year, students can usually move into other housing and this includes fraternity and sorority housing. Enter Greek Life.

Over the years my students have had polar responses to the Greek Life question. When asked if Greek Life is important to them as they search for colleges, it is usually a resounding "yes!" or a definite "no!" Students' perceptions of Greek Life are often that it provides 'guaranteed' friendships and connections. It is a place to belong and live. Other students want no part of Greek Life. I do occasionally have the student who says they do not want Greek Life on campus. I've seen Greek Life make better students and I've seen Greek Life derail students. If you choose to be involved in Greek Life, choose wisely and find something that fits you. Your fraternity or sorority doesn't guarantee you friends or happiness. Only you can do that. Whether you choose to be in Greek Life or not, surround yourself with the people that will be a good influence on you to become the person you want to be.

Socially speaking, the residential halls aren't the only influencers on campus. You must consider the overall vibe of the campus and how it fits you. Whether that be socio-economic dynamics (in other words, money) or school/life balance, we all need time to be social and have a little fun while feeling like we belong.

I enjoy hearing the stories of my students after they return from college visits. When I was still working in the high schools, I could tell by the student's body language as they crossed the threshold into my office whether the visit was good or bad. I tell my students that every school can look good on a website, but you must visit to get the real deal. Website photos depict smiling students, manicured lawns, blue skies, and flowers in full bloom. That's usually a far cry from reality when a student shows up mid-January for a college tour. But most of the time a student can see past the dreary weather to see the school for what it is. Every school has its unique vibe. You can't get that from a website or even a YouTube video. You must experience reality firsthand.

A student of mine had great grades and scores. I mean, Ivy League potential. She was stellar on paper and in person. From the honeycomb perspective, her academic side was firmly rooted in finding a school that would academically challenge her, her financial side was solid as the family had no limitations. Geograph-ically speaking, she was independent, mature, and self-advocating. She would thrive being away from home. She had three sides of her honeycomb firmly in place and finding that top-notch school far from home that would satisfy her thirst for knowledge on every level. One of her family members suggested she visit an exclusive school that, if I told you the name, you would surely recognize. She obliged and headed out on a flight one Thursday afternoon for a long weekend. When she crossed the threshold back into my office on Monday morning, I knew it didn't go well. I could see how deflated (and yet somehow relieved?) she was. When I asked about her visit, there was one thing that sealed the deal that this was NOT her school.

First, she told me about the tour and how well it went. She enjoyed the class she observed and found the material challenging yet felt confident she could handle the rigor. She also liked the professor and the folks she met in the admission office and the student tour guide. The campus was beautiful, and the size was right. So far so good. But then came the deal-breaker. On Saturday evening, she found herself in the room of her ambassador with whom she was staying. The student was knee-deep in books and stressed. She understood her visit might be poor timing, but then she realized that as she walked down the hall that nearly every student was in their room, quiet, and studying. She asked someone if some mid-term exams were coming. The student informed her this was a typical Saturday night. I'm sure she wanted to scream that quote from SNL, "IT'S SATURDAY NIGHT!" It may seem to some who could view this school as their 'dream school' that this was a crazy reason to not pursue admission to this fabulous place. Not only was this student smart, but she was also wise. She knew herself well enough that while she wanted a top-notch education and would work for it, she also sought a school/life balance. She could work hard all week, but she needed to be able to step back at least one day of the week and have some fun. She could ENJOY her college years and work hard to get where she wanted to be. She valued balance and being with friends. She was by no means a party girl, but she needed to step away from the massive stress these students were under—whether dictated by workload or self-imposed. She wanted no part of this life. The Social side of her honeycomb was NOT firmly in place if she enrolled at this college.

While this was disappointing to her, she found her happy place eventually and all was well in the end. Imagine had she listened to the 'shoulds' that she *should* apply there or that she *should* go there. What a stressed and unhappy (and likely unsuccessful) student she may have become had she not considered the Social aspect of her college choice.

Another of my students didn't listen to that vibe or notice things on a campus tour that ended up bringing her back home. Her initial dream was to pursue a degree at an out-of-state college. She did her homework and knew what she wanted—religiously affiliated, knew what degree she wanted, absolutely LOVED the city that the school was located, and she had the brains and maturity to handle being on her own far from home. Finances were an issue, but scholarships combined with aid and her parents' saving for her college tuition made this dream possible. She visited and reported back that "Yep. This is THE one." I took her report at face value and was not surprised when she enrolled for the following fall. What I was surprised by was when I heard she left the following May. Early in the year, she had discovered that the school wasn't a fit, but her parents pushed her to stay the entire year insisting it was an adjustment period or homesickness. I admire their advice. It usually is homesickness or adjustments driving the unconnected feeling the student has. And, after an adjustment period, they usually settle in quite well. But in this case, it was something entirely different. As bright as this student was and capable of living on her own, she failed to pick up on the socio-economic vibe of this college on her visit. As she described it this place was 'polos and pearls.' She said, "And I mean POLOS and PEARLS." The real deal. For her, she was content attending class in her sweats and jeans, but for other students, it was dressy and put together all the time. She didn't mind that she looked different. She chose to dress that way. What bothered her was the conversations she overheard about people name-dropping brand names or criticizing or making fun of others who weren't dressed 'to the nines' like they were. For this student, she didn't feel she fit socially. She felt excluded and judged. The parties and trips and other tangible 'extras' these students possessed were nowhere near what she had and while she didn't feel her life was somehow less because of that, she did feel others negated her worth because of these worldly things. It became hard for her to connect socially and she ultimately returned home. She then re-routed, checked out her options for other schools, visited and paid attention to the social vibe and made a better choice for herself. After successfully transferring, she graduated on time degree in hand. I don't think she ever looked at the experience as a failure. For her, it was a lesson in understanding herself and what was important to her. **Knowing what you value is an extremely important part of the college search process.** She could have let this experience break her—come home and drop out. Instead, she firmed up the Social side of her honeycomb and moved on with her life.

Everyone's comfort level is different, and the social aspect of college is no different. While my previously mentioned student was uncomfortable with the socio-economic dynamics of her initial college choice and felt like a fish out of water, not everyone has the same experience. I worked with a woman who was a great teacher. She was young, energetic, smart, and witty, but she was also very simple; sort of a what-you-see-is-what-you-get sort of demeanor. Unpretentious, raised without a silver spoon in her mouth or any other material benefits in life, she was raised as blue-collar as they come. She was far from spoiled or being into name brands. Her brains got her into a stellar college in the southern part of the U.S.

and she did exceedingly well academically, and it molded her into an excellent teacher. She brought her educational experience and innate intelligence into her classroom every day teaching gifted students. When I had an opportunity to go on a college tour trip that included her alma mater, I was surprised by what I found. From my perspective, this school's students seemed privileged, outfitted in name brand clothes and accessories. While the students and staff were nice, it appeared to me that not everyone might be comfortable in such a surrounding if they didn't come from a similar socio-economic background as these students because the obvious was, well, pretty obvious. These students had money and it showed. I immediately thought of my work colleague and her fairly simple attire (no name brands here), the girl who never put on airs. How in the world did she survive here? How did she ever fit in? How did she find anything in common with other students?

My curiosity got the best of me and I immediately sought her out when I returned from my trip. I felt comfortable enough to ask her point-blank, "How did you end up there?!" She smiled immediately. She knew what I was referencing. She knew she was that proverbial fish out of water. She told me with a big smile on her face that, yes, my perception of that school's social side was indeed accurate. There were mostly privileged people on that gorgeous campus, and she was not one of them. She said it intimidated her for a moment, but she wanted the education and she was not one of those people ever impressed by those with money anyway, nor did she ever allow herself to feel less than because of her modest upbringing. If they didn't like her for her, so be it. She would not be someone she wasn't. For her, the Social side of her honeycomb was not as important as the quality of the education she received. She knew her life here was temporary and these were probably not people she would be friends with forever. Her goal was to receive a good education and the social aspect never bothered her enough to be a deterrent. She was a rare individual who would not feel uncomfortable in the presence of such stark financial differences, but it simply did not bother her. She was as grounded as they come. She found her small group of friends and stuck with them. She enjoyed college, but then she graduated and got on with her life. I think it's all in how you look at things and how you're wired. Most of us need a comfort zone; she was one of the few who didn't. Her Social *why* just didn't factor in as much as the other sides of her honeycomb. And, her honeycomb was still sturdy.

This was quite a different experience for another student who visited an academically strong school that didn't quite measure up socially. Geographically, it was far from home and that was okay. She was academically fit for the school and that was good. Financially, things were a stretch but doable with the right sacrifices that her parents were willing to make happen for the right school (without over-extending themselves or breaking the bank). The sides of her honeycomb were coming together nicely and so her parents arranged for her to visit the campus one fall weekend. Just like with the previous student, I could tell by her body language when she came into my office after the trip, she had not found her dream school. I asked her how it went, and she said it didn't feel like the right place for her. Her perception was that people were not friendly. They seemed competitive and not at all interested in others, but more so in getting ahead. This student was pretty people-oriented and friendly and willing to help anyone, but she didn't connect with like-minded personalities there. Now, I think it's fair to say you can't determine the personality of every student on campus on a two-hour tour. However, I think we all get that 'vibe' of whether we fit in at a given place if we listen to our intuition. As one girl told me when she returned from a visit, "I found my people." She knew she'd found her home. For this young woman, though, this was not her tribe. She did not fit. Her gut told her that. She wanted a great education, but she also needed to feel connected. She was collaborative by nature, and here she told me she didn't feel like people would help her if she asked for it. She said the competitive nature and quest to get ahead were predominant and got the impression these students received substantial pressure from parents to succeed. She felt her values and theirs did not align. She didn't criticize them for that. She just didn't feel like this place was a fit for her. She also felt like the socio-economic factors played a role in the students' pressures and quest for success and that the basis for education was strictly status and monetary. She was intimidated by the stories of their upbringings and lifestyles. She thought she was being a bit too hard on them and adjusted her mindset and give it another chance. But when her host for the visit reported she was leaving for the weekend and the family helicopter was waiting to fly her home, she threw in the towel. She was in over her head. She knew her aspirations for the social aspect of the college experience were not a match for this school despite being a fit on so many other levels. And while this was disappointing to her, it was far better to be disappointed before enrolling and then deciding she didn't fit. She continued to look for a college until she found her people, a place she fit and could call home for the next four years.

While the economic piece of the Social side is important, there are other things to consider socially as well. For example, students must consider their ability to become involved in clubs, activities, and be social in the community. Besides Greek Life, what social supports are there to help life away from the classroom be fun or enjoyable? I'm not just talking about the party scene, but everyday events that encourage students to bond with one another and form friendships and develop values they will use throughout their lives. As part of a counselor tour group a few years ago, I visited a school that encouraged students with common interests to form their own clubs and create a way to have fun with others. In response to this encouragement, our tour guide told us his friends had formed a "Waffle Club" where they got together every Monday night and made waffles and hung out. He told us that about 20-30 students came each week. I don't know about you, but if I were still in college these would be my people!

Being social means different things to different people—Waffle Clubs, Harry Potter clubs, frisbee golf clubs, intramural sports, dodgeball teams. I think it all exists in some form or fashion. And if what you want doesn't exist, will your school of choice encourage you to develop a social outlet? Finding your fit is as unique as the individual. How you connect is so important—from Greek Life to living-learning communities, from clubs and intramurals to study groups and community volunteering. It will serve you well to find a school that will develop that social side of you. It's important to find that place you can grow as a person as well as intellectually. You need to fit your Social *why*. You must do you! No one else can. Having a strong social side to your hexagon will only make your honeycomb stronger. If you encounter difficulty in life while you're in college (and we all do), the social connections that are there to care about you, support you and help you will be key to your survival. Remember, that honeycomb represents a strong student— resilient, successful. You can't be that without the Social piece as a firm foundation on which you build your educational house.

I would be remiss if I didn't address diversity on campus. But I don't want to talk about diversity in the racial sense necessarily. I want to talk about diversity in other ways particularly in thought. It is no secret that in the United States we are constantly bombarded by messages of discord these days. If someone doesn't share our viewpoint politically, religiously, or otherwise we are quick to condemn. Whether in person, at a march, on social media, we are quick to criticize and to judge. College is a melting pot of ideas— some conservative some not; Democrats versus Republicans; Pro-Choice versus Pro-Life; various religious beliefs or attitudes. The list is endless. Safe to say, we are not all going to agree on everything! But I think the college experience can go a long way in helping to open doors of communication between individuals. That's not to say anyone is going to change anyone else's mind but learning to listen and communicate without anger or hate could be powerful stuff. I would encourage folks whose knee-jerk reaction is to enroll in a school they think will never have them encounter a person who thinks differently than them to reconsider. This isn't about changing minds. It's about a lot of other things—listening, communicating, understanding perspectives, and (hopefully) encouraging peaceful endings. College is a great time to open yourself up to discussion, expose yourself to different viewpoints, cultures, religious beliefs, races, socio-economic backgrounds. It's about widening your world and narrowing the gap between us. I encourage you to find a school that opens your world and challenges your brain and belief system. But more so, to find a place that allows you to become a better person—a better listener, communicator, problem-solver. I'm guessing not everyone in the Waffle Club is the same religion or the same political party. They may have different views on homosexuality or balancing the budget. Regardless, they've found common ground in waffles and that's a start. Sometimes when we meet people and bond over simple commonalities—like waffles—we like them because we've formed a connection, a common bond. When we find out they think differently about other more controversial topics, I think it's fair to say we are more likely to give them a chance and hear them out because we already know them. Accept the differences even if we agree to disagree. I doubt anyone left the Waffle Club in a huff because one guy liked blueberries in his waffles and the other guy liked his plain. While the stakes are higher depending upon the topic, maybe we can find common ground in college with those different from us. Maybe it can be a start toward more civilized dialogue.

Why do I bring this up in the social piece of this book? Because as you are looking for a college, be open to finding something that socially might push you out of your comfort zone just a tad. I wouldn't advise that you do a 180 and enroll your conservative self at a full-on liberal campus (or the reverse). You probably wouldn't be happy or thrive in such a drastic change. I would encourage you, though, to find a place that will expose you to a variety of people so you can experience new things while still finding your people— those you connect with. Don't seek a place where every person and every idea are 100% compatible with you though. There are degrees of relationships and acquaintances. People different from you are no different than you being different to them. It's just two sides of the same coin. **Learning comes in many forms and learning about people is just another form of education.** As my dad used to say, "That guy puts on his pants one leg at a time just like me." Look for the common connection first. Even if it's waffles.

Questions to Ask Yourself About Social Fit

- What's the overall 'vibe' on this campus?

- Do I feel like these are my people? Do I connect here?

- How can I grow here socially? Will there be enough people like me while still being exposed to a variety of people and ideas that will help me learn and grow socially?

- Are there clubs, intramurals, living communities, Greek Life, etc. that will allow me to get involved?

- Can I create a club if I want to start one?

- Are there enough students here that are different from me that will allow me to meet others different from myself?

- Does this campus have a strong religious or political vibe that feels uncomfortable/comfortable to me?

- Is there a culture (drugs, alcohol, parties, other areas) that I feel uncomfortable with at this school?

- Is there enough to do in the community at large that I feel a connection there as well?

- Does the dorm or residential hall set-up—communal or suite-style—fit my needs? Does it allow and encourage me to be social while still giving me some space for privacy?

Emotional

The Emotional side of the hexagon along with the Personal side are the last pieces of the honeycomb. I'd like to spend a lot of time here because this is the area considered the least when making a college decision and yet it is an area with a powerful influence on whether students succeed and stay enrolled in college. **College is quite the undertaking and a student's ability to stay focused depends upon not only their academic prowess but the state of their mental health.**

The statistics for mental and emotional health in the United States are astounding. Suicide rates have risen by an alarming rate the past decade both in terms of completed suicides and attempts. More students report having diagnoses for anxiety, depression, and Obsessive-Compulsive Disorder (OCD). More students are on prescribed medicine than ever before. People often ask 'why' about the reasons behind these startling numbers. How did we get here? What caused this? How do we fix this? Those are big questions (and good ones). A definitive verdict isn't in yet, but there is great speculation about the recent introduction of technology to a generation never raised without it. From screen time to social media to isolation and online bullying, many people are pointing the finger at technology as the cause of our emotional upheaval. Some people point the finger at family dynamics while others suggest a lack of coping skills or resiliency. I'm not here to talk about the reason we have these issues, but I would like to address the topic of support for these issues as it relates to college.

With facts like those reported above, we can't ignore that we have large populations of young people who are suffering and need support for mental and emotional health issues. Mental health has to do with how we process information and respond to challenges while emotional health has to do with those feelings we experience because of processing the information. We all have emotions—happiness, joy, fear, sadness—that we identify with and have felt. It's part of being human. To keep denying our emotions is, in my opinion, keeping us from being human. If we ignore or turn off our emotions, how can we ever experience compassion or caring for another? Love? How do we push through scary or uncomfortable feelings to get to something better if we can't acknowledge them?

Mental and emotional health is part of who we are from the time we are born until the time we die. But unlike our physical health which we are encouraged to talk about, address and perhaps even brag about (ever see a car with a 26.2 marathon sticker on the back?), our mental and emotional health does not get the same attention or respect. I doubt we will ever see a sticker on the back of a car that reads, "I kicked anxiety's butt at the therapist's office today." We just don't talk about it. We do not have to talk about it every day with everyone. It's private for sure. Just like going to the doctor about that nasty rash you have is private—some things you just don't want the world to know. **Keeping it private isn't the issue; not doing anything about it is.** We can go to the doctor and not tell anyone, but that doesn't stop us from going to the doctor and getting the help we need to resolve the issue. And, it's probably not even that we are ashamed about it. It's more that it's just not anyone else's business.

Our younger generation is addressing mental and emotional health issues more aggressively than previous generations. They are more apt to seek help or admit struggles. Even the Duke of Cambridge, William, along with Prince Harry has openly discussed the grief they endured as children after the death of their mother, Princess Diana. From sharing their own experiences, they have created an open dialogue about the need for individuals to seek help when they need it. Their role modeling is creating conversations about emotional health that otherwise would likely have gone unspoken. They have taken some stigmas of this topic away.

Recently, I saw a young college-aged woman wearing a shirt with wording on the back. It was one of those tie-dyed t-shirts much like those you'd see worn on any high school or college campus. As I read the back of her shirt, I was impressed by the message. It simply read, "6 Ways 'College X' Students Get Rid of Stress." It outlined how surveyed students at her college handled stress in positive ways. The answers ranged from talking with a friend, exercising, taking a nap, and even eating chocolate. The message conveyed was there were various ways to handle stress without alcohol or other detrimental decisions. I was impressed by the positive message the shirt sent and it seemed to speak volumes about how the college wasn't afraid to talk about mental health issues. It was nice to see they put the issue front and center (or, in this case, on the back) on a t-shirt and didn't act as though stress or problems didn't exist at their school. Remember, there is no "Utopia University". **If you're interested in finding the right fit for yourself, look for a place that seems to have your best interest at heart and wants to help you succeed on**

every level including emotionally. Whatever is a challenge for you in college whether it be stress, depression, or other circumstances, don't let it erode you. Find a professional counselor on campus (or in the nearby community) who can help you before what you're struggling with erodes you to the point of not being able to function. A good college will have those resources to support you emotionally. If we can work to change the dialogue about mental health and emotional issues, then maybe we can encourage others to seek the help they need (and deserve).

And problems not monitored or addressed DO erode us. It's not usually one big event. It's usually a slow, gradual process that, over time, creates a situation where we are far from where we started and far from who or where we want to be. It moves us off our center. Drug and alcohol addictions often work like this. So do other emotional issues (even grief) for which we do not seek an outlet. That's not to say every affliction in our lives requires medication. Often, just the opportunity to seek help from someone who can objectively listen and help us can offset the need for medication or a deeper erosion of ourselves. But, unfortunately, our society has taught us from generation to generation that asking for help is a sign of weakness. I beg to differ.

Remember that presentation I gave to the parent group a few years ago? The one where they asked me to talk about the stress regarding academics and the college process? Some of those students' responses from the survey I gave will always stick with me and remind me we can never truly knew what another person has going on in their life. I had not shared with you previously some of those responses I read that night, but I'd like to share them now. I'd like to share them because they are authentic, and it shows you the emotional stress that students are under.

Some of the comments (or messages) students had gotten from their parents included the following:

"Sometimes they make it seem like all children have to be perfect."

"You can do better."

"Quit telling me to perform to 'academic potential' but then expect perfection."

"They tell me I can't do things if I get lower than a 95."

"They tell me a B+ is basically an F."

"They tell me I won't get into college without good grades."

"They hound me about grades and tell me to work harder when I'm already working as hard as I can."

"I feel like I have to get great grades in order to make my parents proud. I'm always terrified to tell my parents about 'bad' grades because I feel they'll be disappointed in me."

"They don't seem proud of me if I get an average grade even if I tried my best."

"They really don't stress me out in terms of academics. As long as I don't have any B's, I'm fine."

"They compare me to my siblings."

"My whole future is based off what college I get into."

"My parents told me there's not a chance I'm going to get into college."

"My parents ridicule the school I want to go to."

"Please stop telling me I'm a failure."

"It's like a triangle and the points are—social life, enough sleep, and good grades. You can only choose 2."

"Stop yelling!"

"What I fear about the college process is not getting accepted after all the hard work I did in high school."

Whether misinterpreted, self-imposed, or completely accurate, students' real and perceived pressure from parents regarding grades and college is creating stress for them. For most high school students, self-esteem is a major influence. Students who are already hard on themselves (even if you never hear it or see it) and then hear messages at home reinforcing their negative thoughts of themselves are eroding their confidence. A friend had a great saying about how to view people. She said, "You can never compare your insides to other people's outsides." What she meant by that was that while we are generally in touch with our feelings and struggles, we can never know what the other person has going on in life. You might think your own life is a big failure and look at someone else's as a perfection. You might think this because they have a happy social media presence or are always smiling. But you honestly have no clue what's going with anyone because we can't see in their heart and mind. It happened frequently that a student would come to my office at school crying and upset over a multitude of various factors. In processing their feelings, they would inevitably remark that so-and-so has it so easy—they're popular, smart, athletic, etc. But what I saw as a counselor that this student didn't know was that 'so-and-so' had just been in my office the day before sobbing over their parents' divorce, bullying, a break-up, an eating disorder, depression, a bad grade, friend troubles, academic pressures, or a thousand other things. Be careful of wanting what someone else has. You may not fully grasp what you're wishing for.

School counseling offices are often what I call MASH units. For those of you who aren't familiar with a MASH unit (or the popular TV show of the 1970s), MASH stands for Mobile Army Surgical Hospital and it is a place near the frontlines of a war. It is the place where the wounded are brought to be assessed and receive immediate (sometimes lifesaving) care. From there, the more serious cases are shipped out to facilities or resources that can better help them. School counseling offices are just like this. They are the initial intake for students who are hurting—emotionally, academically—and they do their best to assess the situation and provide the student with the next line of care needed. Often, it is as simple as providing the student with an opportunity to talk in a safe place free of judgment. I've had many students over the years find their way to my office, walk in the door, plop down, and sob. I was always grateful for this. My office provided an outlet, and this was their first (brave) step in getting the support they needed. Sometimes it was something in life that had them down like a difference with a teacher, friends, a failed test, or frustrations with mom or dad. It didn't matter to me. I was just glad to provide a place where they could catch their breath and get it all out. Usually the strong emotions they experienced subsided by the end of our conversation or over the next day or two. Many students would come back and just poke their head in and say thanks for being there and let me know today is a better day. I loved that. Maybe it was a lack of sleep or a bad case of PMS that caused an uptick in their emotions. Regardless, it was good they had a place to just vent it out, right the ship, and get on with life.

But for others, the issues were more constant and sometimes due to strong outside forces. Horrible home lives, unrelenting (and sometimes abusive) pressures from parents, depression, anxiety, eating disorders, thoughts of suicide. These more pronounced situations prompt counselors to seek additional resources to help their students. Much like a MASH unit, these counselors need to know when to refer out. Perhaps a student needs an in-patient hospitalization. Maybe they need a counselor or facility that specializes in eating disorders. Or maybe they need a support group for the grief they are experiencing. **A counselor who refers out is NOT one who doesn't want to dial in.** A school counselor who refers out is one who knows their limitations (whether time or experience) to adequately provide a student with the level of care they need. A good school counselor has a strong list of referral resources ready in their back pocket to get their students the next level of care.

Few students get through high school without some issues. For some, situations are resolved with little intervention or long-term care. For others, ongoing support is necessary to keep them afloat and going in the right direction. And for some of those, they might deal with a lifelong diagnosis of depression, anxiety, or other issues for which they may always need support. While many parents are supportive of their students getting help during the high school years, it seems that help is a secondary thought when considering college. Let's say you'd been sick and needed an antibiotic for strep throat. You'd still take your medication while on vacation, wouldn't you? So why do we forget about support services when checking out colleges? If a diagnosis requires medication, such as depression, ADHD, anxiety, or other physical diseases (diabetes, etc.), don't forget to check out resources in proximity to the college that can support you. Make sure there is a pharmacy nearby where patients can pick up prescriptions and ask questions. Many insurance and drug companies will not send prescriptions to PO box addresses, so there must be a pharmacy or hospital nearby where students can get medication if it can't be mailed. The last thing you want is for a student to abruptly stop the medication for any sort of ongoing diagnosis. Imagine for a moment if your student had depression. Perhaps you've been sending the medication with them when they visit home because the insurance company won't ship it to their PO box at their school residence hall. Then there's the one time you forget to order it when they're home or they decide not to come home for a while and they no longer have access to it. And for most of us, we don't think about it until we are out of it. At that point, it may be too late to provide continuous medication without a cold turkey stop. Unfortunately, that can spiral a student out of control quickly. From an emotional standpoint, a student could easily lose a semester or two if they don't have the medication they need and suddenly drop out of life when they find themselves not going to class or getting out of bed. Check out your pharmaceutical resources and lifelines before you pick a college. I don't care how smart you are, you won't be able to perform academically if you can't function because depression has you chained to the bed or living in a constant fog because you're off your meds and you can't access them locally. **If the Emotional side of your honeycomb isn't shored up or supported, it can wreak havoc on your Academic side.**

Besides prescription support services, consider the support available for physical ailments or emergencies—broken bones, emergency appendectomies, etc. Ask about (and visit) the health services department at the college you are considering. What are their hours? What needs are they equipped to handle? If a student has an emergency at 3 am and needs to be hospitalized, does an employee of the college accompany the student or stay with them until a parent or guardian arrives? How is the parent notified if there is a medical emergency? This may not seem like a big deal, but if you have a student with chronic asthma or diabetes or a myriad of other illnesses, you must know someone can be there for them in the parents' absence. Emotional or physical health issues don't just magically disappear after high school and it's important to consider what support is in place to handle those situations should they occur. As much as students want their independence, we all want some support when we aren't feeling well or are feeling vulnerable.

The same is true for those ongoing issues that may not be a chronic physical illness or medicinally supported issues. What about the issues like ongoing counseling? Many students seek assistance for therapy during high school for a multitude of reasons—eating disorders, self-esteem issues, general anxiety, depression—the list goes on and on. Most realized that they had something going on that they needed additional help for if they were going to get on top of this and get whatever the issue was under control. During those formative high school years, they participated in counseling to help provide an additional level of support to get them out of a tailspin or feel better about themselves. Most students went begrudgingly not wanting to admit they could use a helping hand. However, most quickly came to see and rely on the benefits that counseling provided. Some ceased counseling after a while and were stronger for the experience. Others could stop therapy for a time and then start again when they slipped backward or into undesired patterns. Some others required ongoing support and continuous therapy was necessary. **Regardless, if a student still needs or required therapy at any point in high school, they may need that support again.**

During my years working in a high school setting, I noticed students hit roadblocks in certain grades more than others. By far, that grade was sophomore year. Sophomore year is that 'lost year.' The newness and excitement of high school are wearing off, courses are getting harder, and then there is the dreaded 'sophomore switch.' (Sophomore Switch is a time where those who you thought were friends often disappear to other friend groups leaving you in the dust often without any explanation or warning.) It's a tough time for most teens. Unfortunately, this often happens in conjunction with other age-appropriate developmental issues for students. It's when they suffer from academic pressures, self-esteem issues, and an identity crisis. While not all kids in this phase need counseling (but lots of love and patience from those around them), some develop deeper-seeded issues like depression, eating disorders, and cutting. If there's good news in sophomore year, it's those who work at the high school level along with the parents can still have a watchful eye on the student. If something happens in sophomore year that necessitates counseling, we have a couple of years to help them find their way again. But when a student approaches graduation and has an unresolved issue, it can be an uncertain situation. For that student, we are in dangerous territory as they leave the nest, the problem still actively in tow, and move to their new life at college. If the proper support systems are not in place at the new school (and sometimes even if they are), the student will often struggle as they navigate making friends and handling new stresses like figuring out schedules and workloads. With no support systems like counseling established, the students often flounder and revert backward in their progress. And while even a student who seems to have that issue from sophomore year under control, people can slide back a bit when faced with change even if it's a positive change like college. Any issue that can be addressed in high school and gives students a solid foundation for when they leave to venture into the 'real world' is a plus.

I once had a student with a serious issue going on in life that required pretty serious monitoring. (I'll spare you the details.) This all popped up during sophomore year. There were lots of tears, time in my office, meetings and phone calls with parents. The student who started high school as a happy, intelligent freshman was eroding under the pressures (many self-imposed) for good grades and perfectionism. Imagine, then, the feeling of failure when perfection could not be achieved, and the bubble of self-confidence burst. Self-confidence eroded and the downward spiral followed including destructive thought patterns, habits, and choices. After quite a period of denial (trying to keep up the perfectionistic appearance), the student, by the end of junior year, was still denying getting the help needed. I was worried about the long-term effects and was mostly concerned about two things—the pressure that the college process would impose and leaving the safety net of high school with no resolution or progress on this issue. Surely, this experience would have a cumulative and far-reaching effect. This was not a problem that could be outrun in college. I finally took a bold move in a window of opportunity I saw. It happened in a discussion one day when the student was beginning to finally concede some help may be needed that I presented two options. It was simply this, "Do you want to kick this thing's butt now and start college on the right foot or would you rather deal with it after you get to college?" For whatever reason, that was the catalyst for change. The student agreed to treatment the summer before senior year, had some ups and downs in senior year, but the good far outweighed the bad. The student's mother called me about a year after graduation. She told me that things were going well, and the student was happy with the choice to do the hard work in high school before heading off to college. The parent also told me the student realized this was a lifelong problem and would always need to be monitored. While I doubt the problem will ever be 'solved' as the problem was chronic and would require lifelong attention to manage it, I think the student's success in college was amplified by the desire to take control of the problem as much as possible BEFORE and AFTER getting there.

Handling an emotional problem both before and after enrolling in college is key to succeeding in college. We must recognize the struggle may be ongoing. Problems don't stop because of our changing schools. Change alone can open a whole new can of worms especially with anxiety. A few years ago, I met a young woman whose anxiety was so bad that, even with medication and therapy, she was barely functioning in any area of her life that required change. She'd suffered through this experience previously when beginning her high school career in a new place. Once she settled in, though, she got more comfortable as time went on. Unfortunately, high school ends eventually and she would have to start over again as she moved on to an even bigger arena like college. Considering a major life change like college nearly put her over the edge. While she was smart and the Academic side of her honeycomb was sturdy, her Emotional side needed work. Even coming to talk to me about the pending changes in her life as a high school senior was taxing and had her on the brink of a panic attack every time she walked in the door. Gradually, over time and with lots of talking, we found the least of the evils when it came to college—commuting was better than living in a residence hall or taking courses online, a smaller school was better than a bigger school, a medium-sized school was even better. We also discussed other considerations like what major the school would need to have. We had to do all this work before she could even consider VISITING a college campus. And visiting campus was a whole other set of issues! The thought of setting foot on a campus where she knew no one nor her way around was too much. This became a challenge. How could she ever enroll if she never would get out of the car?! In the end, and with the help of her mother, I resorted to some exposure therapy techniques to help her be comfortable with the campus visit. What this meant is she took very baby steps to get her to fully embrace being on campus. Instead of a full campus tour, we started by looking at a map of the campus's proximity to her house. From there, we looked at pictures of campuses online so she could get a sense of the layout and aesthetics of the campus. From there (and this next step took a while), she moved on to going to see the campuses with her mom in drive-by fashion. She never left the car but drove around the campuses to see which one left her feeling the most comfortable. Over several months, she went from a massive fear of college to eventually getting comfortable enough to do a formal college tour and eventually hit 'send' on the college application. I was proud of her for facing her fears. While most of us might not understand her anxiety-provoked fear of change, the fear was real for her—and debilitating. Imagine what that first day of college must've been like for her. It was probably both terrifying and overwhelming. But just like starting high school had been fearful for her, she likely worked through it. Had she chosen to ignore the Emotional side of her honeycomb and force her way to go away to a distant, large university, she would likely have turned around and come right back home. While her example is very extreme, it's clear that every student has a different path based on who they are and we must pay attention to what our individual needs are when choosing a college that's the right fit. My guess is she needed some ongoing support once she got to college to help her transition to this new life. Struggles we have don't just magically go away once we leave for college and may need constant support as is evidenced by this student.

A wise move for families in the college search process is to consider what your student has been through in high school. Issues that presented themselves in adolescence can sometimes follow us into adulthood. I strongly suggest families consider student support services available at or near the campus they will ultimately attend. This tends to be overlooked in the process but is paramount to student success. It's also very helpful for the college's counseling center on campus to know who you are and what issues you are facing. If the student should have any sort of mental health crisis, the counseling team at the college can also be instrumental in helping the student navigate conversations with professors and, hopefully, saving the student the agony of having a substantial drop in grade. Or, help them keep from dropping a course because of a mental health crisis. Families must ask a lot of questions about the college's counseling center before the student enrolls at a school. For example, what resources does the school provide that students can access? By this, I mean services that support them physically like health centers and hospitals as well as services that support them emotionally like counseling centers, support groups, and resources in the community. And, more important, how do you find these resources?

I am part of my community's therapists' Facebook page. It is a closed group that allows therapists to seek referrals for specific circumstances. For example, a therapist might ask for a male counselor who specializes in anxiety and accepts a specific kind of insurance. This allows those of us on the page who could fill a need for someone else's client to be a resource for them. The requests never reveal many details about the client, so their identity is always protected. The requesting therapist then passes along any referral information to the client about any resources they find. I cannot tell you how often a therapist is requesting an out-of-town therapist for a student returning to a college campus in another city. It happens all the time. An example might be that the therapist is looking for an anxiety therapist in the Austin area for a student returning to the University of Texas and has Blue Cross insurance. We are constantly asked to help find referrals for therapists in other cities. Since therapists know therapists, we often can find a connection for the client in the new city and help them to at least initially connect with a therapist they can trust who might know someone else who specializes in anxiety. We are a close-knit group always searching for resources to help others.

The reason I bring this up is so families remember to find a therapist in the student's new community before they go there. If the student is still seeing a therapist in their present community, ask them if they do teletherapy where the student and therapist can connect via a HIPAA-compliant video conferencing resource that can allow the therapist and student to still meet weekly. (This will likely only work if you live in the same state as the therapist practices. Therapists can only practice in states in which they are licensed even if the counseling is done remotely.) I still like face-to-face counseling best and if you do too then ask your therapist for a referral to a counselor in your new community ahead of the move. Or, contact the counseling or student support services offices at the campus and ask them for referrals. (While they can handle many of the needs of students, some families prefer a private therapist off-campus.) Well-connected campus counseling services should have referrals at the ready should you want this option. Whether you choose remote therapy, an on-campus counselor, or one in the new community, this will provide the student with seamless support to transition from their old life to their new one without a lapse in care. If the student is supported emotionally in their new community from the get-go, their Emotional side of the honeycomb will be well-anchored and won't affect the Academic side of their honeycomb which will help to ensure their success as a college student.

And let's not forget about those students who experience a traumatic event in high school for which they've never sought help. Examples of life-changing, traumatic experiences include car crashes, the sudden death of a family member or friend, rape, or other violence. It is not uncommon for individuals who have experienced a traumatic event to have a delayed response to the incident. If you are someone (or you know someone) seeking a college and who has experienced trauma previously for which there was no intervention or support, please consider the importance of mental health resources available to you through the college or the community. And remember, big or small issues aside, college presents a great deal of stress and change for everyone including the smartest, most well-adjusted students. From homesickness to being overwhelmed, college is not always the joyous friend-filled utopia depicted in the movies. More often, it is a time of readjustment and navigation just like high school or any other major life change presents. Any support students can access during this period in their life will go a long way to help reinforce the Emotional side of their honeycomb and make them successful both as students and individuals.

Even if you were one of those students who didn't need or seek counseling services in high school, I encourage you to still know what resources are available at the colleges you're considering. Most students that I have worked with didn't come into high school needing counseling support services, but something popped up along the way that changed all that. Life is messy and unpredictable sometimes. And it can happen at any age. From parents dying or divorcing to developing depression, experiencing bad break-ups, or just losing their way for a time, most students hit an unexpected stumbling block that didn't exist when they started college. Knowing that your college offers counseling services that are GOOD and resources that are SOLID is a great safety net to have just if you need it. A lot can happen in four years.

Questions to Ask Yourself About Emotional Fit

- What support did I need in high school for emotional needs that may still need to be monitored in college?

- What resources does the college offer in terms of emotional or physical health?

- Does the college offer individual counseling as part of their services to students?

- What resources does the college offer OUTSIDE of their offices? How well are they connected to therapy resources in the community?

- Does the college offer support groups?

- How does the college handle emergencies that arise (physical illness or emotional issues) that require contacting the parent?

- Is the private counselor I see licensed to do teletherapy in the state I attend school and is he/she willing to continue seeing me after I start college? If not, can he/she recommend someone in the community I will be attending college?

- Do I need medications from a pharmacy? If so, is there one in town that carries what I need? (Remember, in many cases, you cannot have meds delivered to PO boxes which is what most residence halls use for student addresses.)

Personal

The Personal side of the honeycomb is for all those unique situations that pertain to us as individuals that create situations and influence our decisions when choosing a college. The list is wide and varied here. There are so many nuances and exclusive circumstances that may dictate what could be the next best step for a student that the examples shared here only touch the tip of the iceberg. In all my years as a counselor, I have heard countless stories of individuals whose lives are so complicated and challenging and those with such specific talents or interests leading them to specific schools that can fill that unique need they have. From majors and finances to sports and extra-curricular activities plus family situations and health concerns, those personal attributes needed by each student necessitate they heed their intuition to find a school that will satisfy their circumstances. To ignore the Personal side of the honeycomb might keep that student from developing that key part of themselves that would encourage the realization of their full potential. **Personal or extenuating circumstances can sometimes be the catalyst for the deciding factor in choosing a college.**

One of the most common personal factors I have seen for students choosing a college is playing a sport. Playing a sport in college often complicates the college process. I always tell my student-athletes that when you want to play a sport in college it's as though you must jump through two hoops. First, you must find the college that fits you as a student academically (and where they want you as well). Second, you will want to find an athletic program you feel you fit into and have something to contribute as a player and, in return, the team must have a position for you. This second piece also requires that you not only fit with your teammates, but with the coaching staff. College sports, depending upon the program, can run your life and your athletic family often becomes your family throughout your four years because you spend so much time with them. However, you probably should not base your decision for college solely on your athletic program.

It's not uncommon for students to choose a college based on the coach of their athletic program. I would hear from students all the time how much they loved the coach or the other players in the program when they visited the college. When I would ask about the college itself, I could sometimes get a lackluster response. A shrug of the shoulder and a 'meh' or a 'so-so' response was always a red flag. This is because so many wild card factors could happen that, if the single reason they chose the school disappeared, it might not be enough to keep the student-athlete on campus for the remainder of their education. Some examples? The student who chooses a college based on the coach can be left devastated when (sometimes before they ever get on campus) the coach quits or is fired leaving the student empty-handed when their sole reason for attending was the coach. I had a unique situation once where a student chose a college based on the school fit over the coach she liked at the other university. That coach quit that job and ended up at the college she'd chosen to attend. That was a double win for her! It was a good thing she heeded her intuition and chose the school that was a fit all the way around rather than choosing a college based on just the coach alone.

The second reason I think it's imperative that a student-athlete consider more than the athletics program is because it happens all the time that a student-athlete enrolls in a university for the sport alone and then when they blow out their knee or have another career-ending injury they have no desire to remain at the school as a student and will usually drop out or search for another place to transfer. Remember that the term is student-athlete. Notice the 'student' part always comes first. This means you should be there first for your education *then* for your sport. Not the other way around. If your *why* for attending college, though, is solely athletics then I guess you could argue this point.

Some students choose colleges for other personal reasons such as theater, band, or another extra-curricular activity. I had a student who planned on majoring in the sciences. However, her college of choice, she told me, must have a theater program she could become involved in as a non-major. (Some schools with strong theater programs only allow students majoring in theater to have major roles in performances.) This student had two colleges she was strongly considering, both with equally strong science programs in which she could major. One school did not offer opportunities in show productions to non-theater majors while the other school did. Because the Academic side of her honeycomb was being fed at either school, she ultimately chose the one that allowed her to feed her extra-curricular passion. She knew it would give her an outlet and joy for what she loved to do. She paid attention to the Personal side of her honeycomb and it tipped the scales on her final decision.

Learning disabilities or other diagnoses such as being on the autism spectrum might also tip the scales for college choice. I have had students tell me they know that because of their introverted personality or perhaps a diagnosis such as autism or Asperger's that they feel they're just not ready to go away to college or live in a residence hall. Then others tell me they are ready to be on their own but feel overwhelmed or anxious about living on a large campus or far from their home base and so choose a smaller sized option closer to home. Even within a similar situation or diagnosis, two students can choose two options on where to go. This personal side of the honeycomb is just that—personal—and that is the point I want to drive home. These unique and individual circumstances require a personal choice to dominate. This is not a time to look around and see what everyone else is doing. This is the time to march to the beat of your own drum and make your own choice. Recognize that making decisions right for yourself in no way demands you explain your choice to everyone else. If you and your family have made a well-thought-out decision, you don't have to provide any justification or explanation to anyone else. If people want to judge, that's their business. As my dad used to say, "What anyone else thinks of me is none of my business." What a smart guy.

Some other unique situations influencing people's Personal side of the honeycomb? Let's see. A lot of examples come to mind that I have personally witnessed. Here are just a few...the student who had been in a serious car accident and needed ongoing physical therapy or other emotional or physical support to continue recovery and didn't want to be (or couldn't be) too far from home. The student who had cancer or other physical diseases or circumstances that required the student to remain in town for some time. This student might also have needed medical support in their new college community and must be certain the resources that are available were adequate for their needs. The student whose parent had an accident or illness and they wanted to stay nearby. The student whose parent had relocated for work a couple of years before to another state who now had residency making it an option for them to attend a public out-of-state college for in-state rates and be closer to family. The student whose family tradition was to go to "School X" as every generation has done for the past three and they were excited to continue that tradition. The student who sought religious amenities near or on their college campus. The student with special dietary requirements or extreme food allergies that necessitated they have access to dining amenities that fit their nutritional needs. The student with a specific wish to attend a college with a club figure skating club.

Those are just a few of the many, many personal situations that might influence a student's decision. If you just stand back and look at it, none of those listed as examples are bad reasons to choose a college. That is if the other sides of the honeycomb (academic, financial, geographic, social, and emotional) have all been adequately acknowledged and considered. Sometimes a personal reason for choosing a college can be instinctual—that gut feeling. (One personal reason I never recommend a student follow? The need to attend the same college as his/her boyfriend or girlfriend. While it's a brave step to choose a different school than someone you care about, it is often a healthy one.) Personal reasons can sometimes be catalysts or just tip the scales. The message here is that the Personal side of the honeycomb is uniquely yours to own.

PERSONAL

Questions to Ask Yourself About Personal Fit

- What is the one thing that my college must have to make it complete for me?

- Will I play an intercollegiate sport in college?

- Am I choosing my college solely on one attribute rather than considering the college as a whole?

- Do I have any extenuating circumstances that need to be considered in making my college decision?

- Do I have a learning disability or other diagnosis that requires me to have additional support to succeed? If so, what services will be available at the college I am considering? Am I strong enough at advocating for myself to seek the help I need?

- Is it important for me to have religious amenities/services nearby for my religion of choice?

- What unique aspects of my personal life will influence my college decision?

- What does my gut instinct or intuition tell me about a specific college's fit for me?

- Do I have any red flags when considering a specific college?

Putting It All Together

M any people do not like making decisions and, often, the bigger the decision the harder it is to make. A lot of people (parents and students included) want someone to tell them what to do or where to go. A moment of feeling overwhelmed can suddenly drive a student to give away their power and ask the counselor, a friend, or anyone in earshot, "Where should I go?" and hope for the perfect response that will give them that utopian college experience. Unfortunately, it doesn't work that way. Those who work in college admissions on either side of the desk (high school or college) don't have to live with the decision of where you go to college or what you should be when you grow up, but YOU do. Make it YOUR decision. Would you want someone to choose your prom date or your spouse? Probably not. Don't give away your power or succumb to someone else's influences because you feel you can't decide. Decision-making is a skill set sharpened over time. The more you use it the better you get. It's sort of like exercise for your intuition. You'll learn to follow your gut and your instincts over time and the process will become easier and your intuitional 'muscle' will get stronger.

While the final decision is always the student's, I am always happy to suggest colleges to families just beginning their college search to point them in the right direction for what they *think* they want should they seek my input. But, sometimes, even that can backfire despite my best efforts to be helpful. Once, I had a family come in for their student's college planning appointment. It became very evident this family wanted a list of colleges to check out before leaving the appointment. That's not an uncommon request and I'm happy to oblige with the understanding that this is a jumping-off point and not THE list. In other words, I might suggest schools that MAY be a fit for them after I listen to their laundry list of what they think they want in a school. They will need to visit the schools, check them out thoroughly and then report back with their impressions— too big, too small, too whatever. At that point, we can go back to the drawing board and redirect. Or, if they liked the school then suggest other schools that would be similar so they can compare.

Well, this family completely missed the boat on the message I was sending. Instead of taking this list as suggestions or a jumping-off point, they took it as gospel truth, the end all and be all of colleges. THE college was on this list! Their takeaway from our conversation was that I would tell them what to do and where to go and it would be a wonderful fit with their child enrolling at Utopia University! They did not have any idea of the scope of this huge undertaking of finding a college involved or how much needed to be considered before finding the best fit. With 5,000 colleges in the U.S., we made good progress in our hour meeting to whittle it down to a dozen that could point them toward getting more information and get a baseline of possible schools. It was up to them to visit and decide if we were barking up the right tree or not. I had listened to their 'wish list' of what they wanted in a college—medium-sized, in a small city or large college town, had good school sports and school spirit, had the student's major and would be within 4 hours of home. After listening to their requests, we collaborated to put together a list of schools the student could visit.

A few weeks later, I got a call from the mother. She was loudly proclaiming her disdain for me and the colleges I suggested. One school I had suggested was three hours away and fit the rest of the criteria they requested. I'd visited there personally and had several students who had enrolled successfully and had great experiences there. It wasn't a blind shot in the dark. But there are no guarantees a family will like it and that's why they needed to visit the school and see it for themselves. She told me this one school they disliked so much (I think she used the word 'hated') and that she was calling me because she wanted me to pay for the gas money they spent to travel there and back. (She was serious about this.) I explained to her again this was their decision and that's why they visit—to figure out if it's a school worthy of an application. She wanted none of this. I asked what schools they had researched to determine where else they might consider. She said they had researched nothing because this was 'my job.' She gave away her power. The research, the decisions—it's up to you in the end. Yes, people can assist you in providing direction and suggestions, but no one can do it for you. I knew a very wise counselor once who would never take credit for a student's success in gaining admission to an elite college or winning a prestigious scholarship. Her remark was, "Don't give me any credit because I'm not taking any blame." She got it. She knew her limits. She understood this was the student's journey. Her job was to assist, to co-pilot. She had healthy boundaries. Her job was not to do it all or make anyone's life decisions for them. She would not take on the responsibility for someone else's life direction or take away someone's power to choose their future. Don't give your power away. You may not know what you want to do, but you don't want someone else deciding for you even if it's scary. You know what you need better than anyone.

As for the woman upset with me about not liking the college I suggested, she continued to insist that I pay for THEIR gas because I suggested a school they did not like. She missed the message. She wanted to avoid the responsibility of doing the hard work and wanted someone else to do it for them and then shift the blame when she didn't like the answer. By doing this, she thought she got herself off the hook. But, she didn't. I was not willing to take on that responsibility and neither was she, but this was her child's life and they both needed to take ownership. This is YOUR decision, not mine. Don't look at a bad college visit as a failure or a waste of time. A school whose visit did not go as planned or you did not like is not a bad thing, it's just more information. **Every "no" is moving you toward your "yes."** Rarely do families get the right college on the first visit. I didn't pay for her gas and I am pretty sure I was banging my head on my desk by the time the call ended. I can't remember where the student eventually enrolled, but I remember it was someplace that didn't fit any of the criteria they initially said they wanted. Eventually, they took ownership, figured out what they were looking for, and re-directed.

We are on the hook for our decisions. Our decisions are our responsibility. While others help lead us to the possibilities, it is up to each of us to take charge of our own lives. Own it. Research it. Make your own decisions based on all six sides of that honeycomb. Look at everything—academics, money, location, social, emotional, and personal factors specific to YOUR situation. Don't let someone else call the shots on your life. Decide for yourself. It is, after all,

YOUR life. Your mistakes, missteps, and detours are all yours. Don't fear those, embrace them. It's part of growing up, maturing, and figuring things out. And, it's scary. And you know what? You'll do those scary things and make those big decisions for the rest of your life so you might as well start exercising those decision-making skills now. You'll be doing it for a long time. Just look at all the sides beforehand, so you make a truly informed decision.

That's not to say the Honeycomb Approach means all sides of the hexagon carry equal weight. Just like my work colleague who ignored the Social side of her honeycomb, not every side will carry equal weight. For me, the Financial side carried more weight in the end. For my colleague, the Academic side carried more weight. She was willing to forego the Social side of her honeycomb, but only after careful consideration and an honest assessment of herself that determined it wouldn't have enough bearing on her decision to keep her from going. There are always situations of dichotomous sides of the hexagon that don't complement one another or others that overlap and require some reflection to see which side of the hexagon might outweigh the other. It's through personal reflection that you can look at all the options and decide which sides of your honeycomb will carry the most weight in the decision process.

What would you do in this situation? You are admitted to a top-notch, name-brand school with nationwide name recognition. You get some financial aid, but nothing significant enough to make a dent in the bill. And, by the way, it's your dream school. You also are admitted to a rock-solid program at a very reputable regional in-state public school that has offered you a full ride for the next four years. You won't pay a dime except for room and board. These are your top two contenders. Which school do you choose? For some of you, you're sitting there reading this thinking, "Easy. I'd go for my dream school I worked so hard to get into!" Others of you will think, "That's a no-brainer. I'd go for the free ride." **This is the crux of this whole book—YOU must decide for yourself.** For some of you, the Academic side of your honeycomb might carry more weight. For others, maybe the Financial side wins out. **There is no way all sides of your honeycomb will carry equal weight and that's to be expected. Where the mistake lies is in ignoring or downplaying the significance of the other sides altogether if they truly are deal-breakers.**

As for that last situation I just presented you with, that happened to one of my students. And just for the record, she chose the free ride. Many people disagreed with her, but she knew money was not something her family possessed, and she felt the Financial side of her honeycomb pulling her more. She heeded her intuition, enrolled in the state school, and everything worked out. By the time she graduated, they offered her a full ride for graduate school, and she was quite the graduate assistant running many aspects of the program at the school. After that, she left college debt-free and is having a successful career in her chosen field and living with her spouse in another state. That was her choice. That may not be yours and either choice could be the right one depending upon your needs, wants, and situation. I've seen plenty of families choose to take second and third mortgages on their homes to put their child into their 'dream school.' While I don't advise that, it is ultimately their decision to make. Just like the example of my student above chose the free ride. It was her decision to make regardless of what others thought. Just realize you must live with your decision and the consequences or choose another path to re-route if it's not coming together as you planned.

You might even realize your initial decision wasn't in your best interest. If that's the case, you can still change course and get to where you want to go. When I was at the community college, a guy I knew from high school ended up in my class. He was a year ahead of me and had gone to a strong academic state school a few hours away the year prior, so I was surprised to see him walk into one of my classes on the first day. I asked him what he was doing there. (I thought maybe he flunked or partied his way out of school, but I didn't want to assume.) He told me that while he loved his previous school, it had gotten too expensive for his family. Among other things, he'd gotten involved in a frat and the additional costs were exorbitant for him. He told me that one night he sat in his dorm room pondering the costs of Greek life alone and he said the frat dues worked out to about 7 dollars per friend in the house. He said cheekily, "Then I realized, why pay for friends when I can come home and go here and have friends like you for free?" I laughed but didn't know (and still don't) how to take his remark. Regardless, we stayed friends for a time and he eventually got his degree just like I did. He was smart enough to realize that the decision to go away wasn't in his best interest and re-routed to a more suitable path. He re-routed when he saw the Financial side of his honeycomb had to outweigh the Social. I admire him for doing that. It takes courage to admit you need a do-over. Just like my earlier student who decided her school wasn't a fit after all and dared to admit it, a do-over is sometimes necessary and is never a failure. She tried something she thought was right and when it wasn't, she re-directed and still got where she was going. Just like those many paths to the airport, there are many paths to college.

I've worked in schools and on boards where each one of us took a different path through college. Some were Ivy-educated and some were locally educated. Some traveled abroad and some did not. Some were first in their class and most were not. Some had free rides and some had student loans. Some played sports. Others did not. Some commuted. Others lived in dorms. Yet here we all are sitting in the same meeting, on the same board, or sharing the same employer. **There are many paths to get to where you want to be. Choose the one that is best for YOU, work hard, and you will get where you want to go.**

If you follow the crowd (and many do), you risk falling short of your goals. Students who enroll at the state university because 'all my friends or going there' when they'd be better served with a fresh start out of state is taking a risk. Just as is the student who chooses an expensive, distant school for which they have no financial resources. Or the student who continues to ignore the fact the school is not socially, emotionally, or personally a fit or have no desire to leave home (but do so anyway). They are all making risky decisions. These decisions are risky when based on others' decisions that might not reflect decisions right for YOU. **Emotional peer pressure can be a strong influence when choosing a college and one you must be aware of before it sneaks up on you.** Frequently students will tell me they chose a certain school because they didn't know what to do and wanted to be in the security of friends or familiar territory. (If you remember, I was no different in my initial plan to choose a college.) The problem with this thought process is that you are not considering all the sides of the honeycomb as they relate to YOU. It's hard to imagine in high school that the friends you spend so much time with may not be the friends you have 10 or 20 years from now. That's sad to think about, but it happens more often than you realize. **The only person who will be with you your entire life is you.** It's better to concentrate on what is best for you and not get caught up on someone else's path. Because if you do that and the other person selected wisely for themselves, chances are their best path is not your best path.

I worked with a student recently who remarked on the ambitious nature of her friend when applying to colleges. While my student was looking at great colleges right for her and her dreams, she didn't envy her friend's path. She simply told me that her choices were so 'her' and that she was excited for her friend and what she would be doing after graduation. I found it refreshing that she could forge her own way with all its uncertainties and unknowns and still be happy for her friend who was carving her path to suit her. **It is truly about fit for the individual.** We don't all want the same things in life. Why not be happy for people and let them be happy for us? You might find that even though you take a different path, you may still end up at the same employer, in the same line of work, or even on the same board. Each of you can be equally successful in your unique way despite having taken different routes, enjoyed different experiences, and now bring unique ideas and contributions to the professional circle you share.

Closing Thoughts

There are a lot of messages you can take away from this book—everything from the importance of looking at all the sides of the honeycomb when making a college choice to the imperfections of life and the importance of simply trying your best. While there is a lot to ponder here, I hope you also embrace the notion of failure and the upshot of such an experience.

At my former counseling office, there was a whiteboard with a variety of colored dry erase markers that clients and counselors alike were encouraged to use. On it, they would share pearls of wisdom or motivational thoughts for those coming in and out of the office to read. One day as I was walking by, the word "FAIL" in red capital letters caught my eye. At first, I thought it was an unusually dire message compared to the usual inspirational rhetoric posted there. As I looked closer, though, I saw what it did read: "F.A.I.L. = First Attempt In Learning." That quote created a paradigm shift for me in how I view my failures in life.

We often have such a negative connotation of the concept of failing. That it is something to be avoided. Failure is part of the process of life. It is a powerful teacher. Parents are often misguided to think that children should not fail: Protect them. Skip steps. Don't hurt their feelings or see them cry. Don't punish them or have consequences for actions. However, it is truly the easy way out. It protects the parent way more than the child. When children are not allowed to fail, it gives them a false sense of security. We have bulldozer parents clearing the way; pushing every obstacle from a child's path. It is a short-term solution that is a set-up for long-term consequences. Consequences include the inability to handle disappointment or develop on any level a sense of grit, perseverance, or resiliency.

In a side discussion with my personal physician on a routine doctor's visit, I discovered just how over-reaching the arms of parental involvement have gotten. She shared with me stories of her friends who still teach at the institution where she went to medical school. They expressed their frustration with getting calls from students' parents' attorneys regarding their grades. I almost fell off the exam table when she told me this! Even in medical school, parents were still calling to meddle in student's academic lives going so far as to threaten lawsuits if certain grades were not given! All of this was to shelter their 'children' from negative experiences or working through their issues with a teacher.

When parents shelter their students from negative experiences, I often find students are exceptionally hard on themselves in the college process. Perhaps this undue pressure comes from them witnessing their parents' bailing them out or 'fixing' their academic issues. The expectation that there should be no rejection in the college process is simply impossible. Most students have rejection from one or more 'dream' school. But you won't know unless you try and each rejection, each of those 'no's', is leading you to your YES! I have witnessed students who mourned a rejection from a school (and the rejection could have been from an admission standpoint or the lack of a financial award that made it possible for them to attend), sullenly approached the runner-up school only to find once they got there that this was indeed their dream school, their people, their home for the next four years. I've also seen the reverse. Students who approach the college process with blinders on, who refuse to consider other options when the window of exploration is present and have tunnel vision that the one college they have in mind is the ONLY one that will suffice. Upon enrolling, however, the reality is far different than the image they had created in their minds. Because they declined their right to explore other options, they sit in their rooms, miserable that the college is not living up to their expectations and wondering if they'd been happy elsewhere. This often results from the student not considering other factors in the college admission process. All the factors we've explored as part of this book—academic, financial, geographic, social, emotional, and personal—are parts of the sum of who we are and crucial to making a good college decision.

Even then, there are no guarantees in life. You can do everything right in your college search and may still have to re-route. A redirect may come from an unforeseen circumstance like a family illness or a failure to consider one aspect of your honeycomb that derails your college experience. Either way, embrace any obstacles and mistakes along the way and put them to good use by learning the lessons they present. These lessons are pivotal points in our development regardless of age. Everyone has made a mistake or wish they'd done something differently. An error in judgment doesn't define us, but it makes us stronger if we allow it. These mistakes are there to teach us and not to punish. At some point deadlines necessitate we take a chance, decide, and know we did our best.

Mistakes can happen, but what's important is that you do your best. That means making an informed decision to the best of your ability. Using the Honeycomb Approach can ensure you make a fully informed decision by looking at all sides (academic, financial, geographic, social, emotional, and personal) to determine what is the best course of action for you. Besides considering all sides of your honeycomb when making your college decision, here are a few reminders to help you get where you want to go:

First, it is paramount that you know yourself and give yourself plenty of time to change your mind as you figure out what scenario after high school might fit you best, so **start this process early before you have your back to the wall and deadlines loom.** The process is way more than just filling out forms and visiting colleges. The Honeycomb Approach requires reflection and knowing yourself. This can be hard work, but if you're willing to do the hard work, the payoffs can be tremendous in the end. Don't be that student who follows the crowd. Be that student who finds what is right for YOU regardless of what others think or say. Maturity is a key factor in being brave enough to seek your path. You should be working on who you are and the person you want to come throughout your life. Starting early in your high school career to know yourself will go a long way in making a healthy college decision.

Second, **remember we all come from different starting blocks.** Maybe you don't have the financial advantage someone else does or maybe you don't have the intellectual ability of your best friend to gain admission to that superior school. You may have an advantage in one of your starting blocks that someone else doesn't have. Also, having a starting block advantage such as financially or academically can be a curse. Some students have so many doors open to them because their parents can afford to send them anywhere or because their intellectual capability will open those doors, that they sometimes find themselves overwhelmed. The pressure and expectation to find the 'perfect' school can be almost paralyzing for these students. If your path has been more clearly defined because of other limitations—major, geographic location, ability to get into certain schools—you might consider yourself lucky. You might find your way to your 'yes' a bit quicker than those who have too many options to consider. These students might also find that because of their advanced starting block financially or academically that they experience great pressure from family to live up to a certain expectation even if it means attending a school that looks good but doesn't make them happy.

Also, don't forget to consider your social, emotional, and personal needs. These are the things that make you unique. Paying attention to these individual needs will go a long way in ensuring your post-secondary educational experience will be a good one. Don't ever apologize or sell yourself short. Take good care of yourself! Remember, the only one who will go through your entire life with you is YOU! Find what works for you and make no apologies for creating a future that will ensure your success. As you've probably heard repeatedly throughout your school years, "Keep your eyes on your own page!" No one can do a better job of making decisions for your life than you can. No one knows you better than you know yourself. **Don't give away your power.** Do seek the help of others—counselors, admission reps, tutors, and the like to help keep you informed of the ins and outs of the process and to help you understand options, timelines, and requirements of the college admission process. They are a wealth of information, but don't let them be the ones responsible for your decision. Again, don't give away your power. Take the information provided, do additional research, and make your own decision.

Next, **don't come from a place of competition.** When we come solely from a place of competition, it naturally dictates we must have a winner and a loser. Jealousy never looks good on anyone. Forget keeping up with the Joneses and don't worry about impressing others or caring what they think. Don't let others determine your worth. Who you are is determined by your efforts and hard work, not by the status of the institution you'll attend. **You are enough by your mere existence.** Be happy for others and wish them well on their journey and then focus on your own. The important thing is that YOU are moving forward. Consider your starting block and what opportunities are available to you at this point in your life. Start wherever you are and continue to move forward. **Remember that forward movement creates upward mobility.** But you also must remember that if forward movement eventually creates upward mobility, it will probably involve climbing a hill that may, at times, feel more like a mountain. Regardless, you need to acknowledge that forward movement will involve hard work at some point.

Finally, **run your own race.** This is about YOU becoming the best version of yourself possible. What this means is you will need to embrace your talents, listen to your gut, and move forward—even with some fear or trepidation. Rarely does a large life decision ever come smoothly without some butterflies in the stomach or some outright fear. Fear doesn't necessarily mean you are making the wrong decision. It often means it's just a natural reaction to big change. For example, if you are fearful about living away from home for the first time, that's completely natural. What would be a mistake is if you let that temporary fear keep you from moving forward towards something that might be a great experience for you. Fear is often confused with excitement. Do a gut check the next time you feel a bit anxious or fearful about something. Is it truly fear or is it mixed up with some excitement as you contemplate a change?

Also, don't limit the techniques you've learned from the Honeycomb Approach to just the college search decision. The Honeycomb Approach can help you with that forward movement not only in terms of choosing a college, but the paradigm of this approach can be shifted to help with other aspects of life that require deep consideration in looking at all sides to make an informed and thoughtful decision. As an example, one might use this concept of a honeycomb to explore six sides of a career decision. In this example, the considerations might be the level of education, income, lifestyle, geography, well-being (stress, etc.), and other personal factors (job security, career growth, and work/life balance).

The Honeycomb Approach is a model that can be extrapolated and used in a variety of circumstances throughout life. By doing this, it allows the individual to look at all sides of major decisions and consider the consequences before committing to a specific path. This is a great way to learn to exercise your intuitional 'muscle' by following your gut instincts regarding the information you've gathered and be thorough in your decisions. Don't just limit the use of the Honeycomb Approach to college decisions. Create the sides of your honeycomb following the various aspects you need to consider when making a large decision. While not every side may carry equal weight in the decision-making process, consideration of these factors might make for a well-rounded decision that fits you best.

As you think about all the decisions you'll make throughout your life, let's focus the end of this book where it began. The idea that if we consider all six sides of the hexagon in making a college decision that it will make each student's honeycomb secure. By doing this, it will produce strong, resilient, and competent people capable of being problem-solving, thriving, and successful individuals. Isn't that what we all aspire to be? Taking it one step further, imagine if everyone chose a college or a future that fits them best. Imagine the possibilities! Honeycomb upon honeycomb, stacked solidly together gives the world that is our hive strength. Imagine what a fortress of strength, fortitude, and resources we could produce. By making the question not "where did you go?" but rather "who did you become?" we could completely shift the dynamic of what success looks like.

Who will you become?

Acknowledgments

I would like to take this opportunity to thank everyone who has been supportive of my journey in creating this book. My friends and family who took part in cheering me on, providing feedback, and believing in me are the reason this book exists. It is scary to take on new projects and put your most personal efforts out there for all the world to see. Being vulnerable is not easy, but necessary in becoming who we want and are meant to be. Thanks to all of you for embracing my crazy ideas and believing in my message that we all have something to offer this world if we only have the courage to heed the call.

I only hope I can return the favor one day.

Made in the USA
Monee, IL
03 December 2019